So We May Breathe Free

AVOIDING INEPTOCRACY

Michael Swartz

I0447855

Ineptocracy: *A system of government where the least capable to lead are elected by the least capable of producing, and where the members of society least likely to sustain themselves or succeed are rewarded with goods and services paid for by the confiscated wealth of a diminishing number of producers.*

- Urban Dictionary

To Danielle:

Your generation is the reason I write this, and even though we don't always see eye to eye on everything, it's all done with love.

Table of Contents

1

Introduction

My name is Michael Swartz. I was born and raised in northwest Ohio, and up until the tail end of 2008 I worked as an architect in Salisbury, Maryland, a place I moved to in 2004 seeking economic opportunity. Now, by hook or by crook, among the jobs from which I scratch out a living one is that of a freelance writer.

Obviously that's not the resume one would expect from a political pundit, nor is it one you'd foresee as a man who deigns to write about the future of America. Three years ago I wouldn't have thought I had this book in me because most people who write these sort of tomes hail from high elected office or work for a political think tank. I possess neither of these attributes; however, I am a bit of a student of history and more importantly I keep a copy of one of the finest documents ever crafted by mankind's hands close by the laptop I write on – The Constitution of the United States.

In writing this book, my goal is very simple: persuade readers that returning to the values which made our country the best place to live in the world (or as Ronald Reagan liked to refer to America, the "shining city on a hill") is necessary for our nation's survival. I caution, though, that the return will be a long-term process.

Since this is indeed an introduction to most of you, I suppose it's best to work in a little background on who I am and what I'm about. Despite the fact I'm not a well-known political pundit, I do have some experience in both worlds.

While I've always had some interest in politics, the reason I became more active in the political realm was simple: I saw it as a way to make a difference. It was just after my thirtieth birthday that I accepted an invitation to join my hometown's Young

Republican Club. At the time I was young, idealistic, and certainly willing to learn, but unfortunately had not a clue how to accomplish what I wanted to do. As I got older and more experienced in the political world, I learned much more about those assets I consider my strengths and those areas where my weaknesses lie, and tried as much as possible to manage my life to bypass those skills in which I'm least proficient.

Thus, while I had thoughts and a little bit of ambition for seeking an elected office such as a seat on the city council or as a state representative, one thing I found out rather quickly after getting involved is that I'm by no means the prototypical politician. I don't have a snake-oil salesman's gift of gab and the part about raising money and saying what I think people want to hear in order to collect their votes doesn't appeal to me very much either, at least in a large-scale sense.

On the other hand, I found an ability to put words to paper or onto a computer screen, words that can become a good argument for the position I'm advocating. Indeed, political movements have room for people with my particular talent so I've been graced with attracting notice from various people and getting opportunities that not just anyone can take advantage of. Back in my era of political nascence, I helped with the newsletter for our Young Republican club and would write the occasional letter to the editor of my local newspaper.

Where my political punditry phase really got its start, though, was with my being accepted to write on an occasional, anonymous basis for the *Patriot Post*, an online newsletter. Naturally, that whetted my appetite for exposure and soon I found a new outlet, the up-and-coming trend at the time called blogging. While my site, called monoblogue, is not yet the most successful or well-read political site out there, it's still worked better than I thought it might have when I began it back in late 2005. From there, it led to other opportunities such as becoming a syndicated op-ed columnist and being featured on a number of nationally recognized websites. It's a job which entails a lot of reading, and obviously I stay current with the political trends this way.

Even though the political climate ebbs and flows on what's seemingly a daily basis, I feel that there's going to be more to this modest but blossoming success of mine and I'm led to believe it's because I put together a political website and other writings which don't go into the personal attack mode many others do. Further, when I write about a problem, more often than not I have some thoughts or suggestions for a solution to this issue. Much of this book can trace its origin to posts I made on my website, writings that I've supplemented in putting together the volume you're reading now.

And this in turn brings me to what I'm going to attempt to begin in these pages.

When I ran for my current post on my county's Republican Central Committee, my main goal was to make it a county where Republicans outnumber Democrats. In this case we needed to convince about 2,000 voters to switch parties. In my mind, part of achieving this goal was figuring out how to get the younger people here to become more active in the conservative movement, for it's my belief that it's in their best interest to follow conservative principles and that American society will be more successful in the long run once they do.

So far, though, it's been tough sledding at best – in fact, we've actually lost a little bit of ground since I was first elected in 2006. But I don't see the problem as being one of conservatism. If anything, the GOP both in my small home county and nationwide has suffered because of the lack of fidelity to the conservative principles which made it the reasonable alternative to the pervasive liberalism and growth of government we've seen over the last century.

If people who are naturally inclined to vote for conservative values see a situation where neither alternative is satisfactory, they'll lose interest, stay home on Election Day and perhaps switch over to an inactive, unaffiliated status. Fortunately, a large number of these people got back into the game and have moved politically to become the backbone of the TEA Party movement. In fact, after losing registration ground over the final few years of George W. Bush and the hope and change of Barack Obama, since 2010 voter registration growth for the local GOP has handily outpaced that of Democrats in my rural county, reflective of a national trend.

Also, as we saw in the 2008 election, the youth responded well to the positive message which Barack Obama spoke so eloquently well. Unfortunately, he didn't go into many specifics but "hope" and "change" turned out to be fair enough buzzwords to secure about 2/3 of the youth vote. Obviously the perception that conservatives are fuddy-duddies had successfully permeated the youth thanks to the mass media's portrayal of "right wing extremists," those who in truth represent the bedrock citizens which make this republic work. But we're really not that uptight, and this is another item my book will attempt to dispel – for the most part. There are some issues you just can't be mirthful about.

I noted earlier that I was not born to be a politician because my skill set isn't the same as, say, a Sarah Palin, a Bill Clinton, or even a Herman Cain. Sometimes it's disheartening to realize this because I think I have a lot of good ideas.

But it can be liberating as well. Since I'm not a legislator or seeking an executive-type post, I don't have to deliver a lot of hollow promises. In fact, my political philosophy may turn some people off because I'm the sort who doesn't believe that government in and of itself should enrich people nor do I think it's a proper vehicle for wealth transfer. Unfortunately, it's been noted that "a democracy...can only exist until a majority of voters discover that they can vote themselves largesse out of the public treasury." Since I'm opposed to that concept, there's no way in hell I could be truthful about my beliefs and ever reach a high enough office to put these plans into action – at least not in the present-day political climate. And while that sort of double-talk and obfuscation is associated with those on the Left, I have no plans to switch parties and become a Democrat. I imagine that move would be the ultimate in reverse psychology.

In some small way, by writing this book I'd like to help be a part of a movement much as the Founding Fathers did at our nation's birth. In more recent times portions of my goal have been accomplished by leaders like Ronald Reagan and Newt Gingrich. Unfortunately, President Reagan is no longer with us to lead but Gingrich continues to write and speak with a similar eye on the future of America. Except for the few months Newt was active in his unsuccessful 2012 Presidential bid, he wasn't shackled by having to pander to an electorate; instead, it freed him to state his case for a movement. As a matter of fact, the reason he bowed out of the 2008 Presidential race was to maintain control of the American Solutions group he founded months earlier. And whether or not you agreed with the concepts or his more recent political missteps, it's difficult to deny the Gingrich vision embodied in the 1994 "Contract With America" radically changed politics in our country.

And therein lies the reason I'm laying this out as a fifty year plan. As I see politics today, it's going to take five decades and at least two dedicated generations to turn back the tide of government that's become one by the elites, for only a selected few, and taken from others – particularly taken from those who achieve financial success. Indeed, it's possible I may not live to see that day my plan would come into full fruition, and there's always the threats from both within and without which could doom American society as we have come to know it.

The chapters you'll read through discuss a number of issues I feel are of paramount importance to the nation's survival. Some issues have very obvious, painless solutions that won't take a lot of hard work to achieve, while others will require generational shifts in attitude and the intestinal fortitude to reverse decades of tradition and law. A few of them may surprise you and ones I've omitted may leave the reader scratching his head and wondering how I could miss such an important topic. It's a case of one man's passion not matching another man's – for example, with the 2007 I-35W bridge collapse in Minnesota our nation's infrastructure became a topic in the 2008 election. Afterward, "shovel-ready jobs" became a pillar of President Obama's economic stimulus plan – one which was supposed to focus on public works but instead turned out to be more like something you shovel out from behind the horses in the parade.

In my case, I think the solution to the infrastructure problem is relatively cut and dried. One giant and immediate step toward solving the problem would be to stop spending as many tax dollars on mass transit few people ride and bike paths that only hardcore bicyclists traverse and shift those funds to more important items like repairing bridges and widening roads to alleviate traffic bottlenecks. Much as bureaucrats and socialist central planners would like us to change our transportation behavior to suit what they feel is best – especially ones who still adhere to the faulty notion of anthropogenic climate change – most of the rest of us just want to get from point A to point B with as little hassle as possible. Thus, a simple answer: build roads which are built to last decades, with more carrying capacity.

There you have it – one solution, one paragraph. And no need to burden consumers farther with an increased federal gasoline tax.

In all candor, though, the example I use is definitely oversimplified. I just don't feel that as a societal problem infrastructure rises to the level of those I take a longer look at in this book. (It's also something which can be better handled on a local or state government level, another important factor in rightsizing government.) Not all of the solutions I propose come simply, but I retain my faith in common Americans to grasp the nation's issues and come up with creative answers which don't always involve the behemoth entities of government.

I have one cautionary note to pass along, though. As I was born right on the cusp between the Baby Boomers and Generation X in 1964, I believe it's likely too late for either of the generations I'm identified with to make a significant change in America. We're quite set in our ways and far too many of my peers have come to depend on government to provide all of their solutions.

I believe our hope for change begins with the Millennial

Generation, those born after 1980. As elders, we can do our part to begin shepherding them in the proper direction but they'll be the ones doing the heavy lifting. This group came of age with the stained blue dress and 9/11, and it's the one who's bearing the brunt of the sacrifices in our overseas conflicts. It's for them that I begin this book, which I'm dedicating specifically to the member of the Millennial Generation I helped to raise. Something tells me that she and her cohorts are more than willing to meet the challenges we face.

2

Community

There are a fair number of subjects I'm going to discuss in this book, but I've decided to begin with a look at what I call community. This isn't a topic which is necessarily political or issue-oriented, but more about what I feel is missing in the present day and yearn to see come back. America in the modern era is certainly the paragon for mankind insofar as our wealth and lifestyle are at a level never seen before in human history, but along the way we've lost some of those things which made our country outstanding and unique in the first place.

Many years ago I wrote a short essay called "Giving Back" for inclusion in the newsletter my former Young Republican club did at the time I was involved with them. While I no longer have a copy of that particular document for easy reference, I still recall the main points and that's what I wanted to base this chapter on, discussing how we've lost our way and how we can pick up the trail again.

For as long as I can recall State Farm Insurance has gone by the slogan, "Like a good neighbor, State Farm is there." While the tagline turns out to be a good sales pitch for a successful corporation, I also see that slogan as a commentary on being good neighbors. Despite all of its problems, America remains blessed with the First Amendment freedom of the people "peaceably to assemble." Across the political spectrum – whether TEA Partiers, Wisconsin union protesters, or Wall Street occupiers – recent days have certainly seen millions taking advantage of this right. Given the rancor which has often occurred at these gatherings, though, some may question the peaceable aspect.

Unfortunately, even with these mass protests, the problem in today's society is people tending to insulate themselves from group settings as much as they can. Many of today's teens (and a surprising number of older folks) interact with each other through Internet sites like Facebook, Twitter, or Pinterest instead of doing what my generation did in their youth. For us, the local mall or the main drag in our small town was the prime hangout spot. Prior to that, generations past would gather after school or on weekends at the local malt shop or sock hop. Regardless of where these societal interactions occurred, they were a part of normal life.

This trend is even reflected in housing. With a background in the architectural business, I notice this more readily but it's also a function of houses I've resided in. In my case this is a total of perhaps a dozen houses which were built anywhere between 1897 and 1978. (Yes, I've moved around quite a bit. It's another function of our more mobile society as well as hard economic times.)

Four of these houses were built prior to World War II and each had fairly similar traits. All were relatively close to the street and had at least some covered front porch attached to them. That style was quite common among the houses along their particular streets and encouraged neighborhood interaction. People would sit out on their front porches during summer evenings and visit if they saw a neighbor outside. During days of yore when most mothers still stayed at home, the women would talk across the fence as they hung laundry out to dry and gossip about neighborhood affairs. After school let out the children would play in the streets until dinnertime, then return afterward until darkness fell and the street lights came on.

Conversely, the commonality among the newer houses where I've resided is a lack of street presence. Only two have had more than a small set of concrete steps in front and, among those two only one had a covered porch. Most were far away from the street due to setback zoning requirements adopted in recent decades and had their outdoor family gathering areas at the rear of the house, generally either a concrete porch or a deck.

This design trend reflected the greater societal push away from interaction and toward enhanced privacy. The newer houses also featured larger yards and were a greater distance from the city core; in other words, typical post-World War II suburbia. Instead of taking the bus or subway to work, commuters spend hours a week in their cars driving to their jobs as development spreads further outward from the original downtown, taking jobs with it. Many commuters now drive around the fringes of the metropolitan area, living in one suburb and commuting to a job in another. This trend also shows the weakness of a hub-based mass transit system which still presumes most people work in a city's central business district.

In the last two decades or so some architects have questioned the role of housing in the community and an urban design trend toward restoring a central core has emerged. While in some cases "New Urbanism" has devolved into an anti-sprawl screed, I still think there are benefits to this type of community. Housing based on those principles takes up less open space and the expense of expanding infrastructure is reduced. Toward that goal, local zoning codes are beginning to recognize that subdivisions which now spread out the houses and push people farther apart may not necessarily be the best use of land.

This push for a New Urbanism gives me the opportunity to reflect on growth as a topic. Obviously as someone formerly in the architectural business my livelihood depended on people building and improving everything from their individual domiciles to entire areas of cities. In my view, there's plenty of room and reason for a moderate amount of restrictions – placed at the local level, by people most familiar with the situation on the ground – in order to make the community as a whole a better place to live. Most zoning codes are based on logical premises; after all, plopping a business development in an area neither easily accessible to those who would be served by it nor where infrastructure can be readily upgraded makes little sense as an investment or to the community as a whole.

There is a point at which I draw the line, though. Some states go too far in restricting uses away from specific areas, or add so many layers of regulation that it becomes impossible for certain types of development to come to fruition. Add in the myriad laws applied by federal mandate, particularly in areas west of the Mississippi River, and sometimes I wonder how anything can get built. It's an issue to me when the rights of spotted owls, snail darters, or caribou stand in the way of development which can improve the area in which a prospective site lies.

Meanwhile, a squeeze occurs from the other direction as a number of private interests have jumped on the anti-growth bandwagon. Citing the mantra of "smart growth," a number of anti-sprawl organizations have sprung up over the last few decades. One umbrella group is the Smart Growth Organization (SGO), which is comprised of a number of governmental and private entities. The SGO includes such diverse groups as the American Farmland Trust, Congress for the New Urbanism, Environmental Law Institute, National Trust for Historic Preservation, Rails To Trails Conservancy, The Conservation Fund, and the Urban Land Institute, just to name a few. All of these groups lobby to reduce the incidence of urban sprawl and preserve land, which in and of itself isn't a completely bad thing.

The problem lies with the most radical amongst these groups who wish to stop growth altogether. Not only would that place all of those in the building professions out of work but it also would eventually preclude the idea of capitalism as a whole, which is why a number of onetime Communists, most notably former Soviet leader Mikhail Gorbachev, have moved to the forefront of radical environmentalism. It is on that fringe where some envision the return of vast swaths of our nation to a wilderness state, with wildlife corridors supplanting human activity in these zones. Another danger posed by these groups and their supporters is the preclusion of individual private property rights for the supposed good of society, a subject I return to and expand on in a later chapter.

It seems to me that we can grow prudently and to the benefit of all if we keep things at a local scale as much as possible. As in most cases, the higher up and more removed government is from the people it affects, the greater tendency there is to enact a one-size-fits-all solution to every problem. I happen to believe that most among us have plenty enough common sense to know what's right for our communities – naturally there are those of us who are perhaps too driven by greed and pursuit of the almighty dollar, but if a generation is instilled with the proper perspectives, values, and ethics this tendency can be kept in check.

And that brings me back to the main point of this chapter. While we can't just tear everything down and start all over, it seems to me that we as a society need to get away from being aloof and self-centered and get back to being more neighborly. The example I used about housing style just serves as a metaphor for what's happened to us over the last several decades. We've become a nation which allows the 2% of bad apples to dictate how we interact with each other. By moving our collective selves off the front porch and out of sight, we've insulated ourselves from the benefits of community.

People in my neighborhood most likely wouldn't know me just from writing this book. But if I tell them I'm the guy who they see on his walks up and down the neighborhood streets several times a week they may say, "okay, now I know who you are." When the weather is warm and more people are outside they recognize me and wave or say hello. My neighbors have come to realize that I'm not out walking around to case their house for a burglary or looking to kidnap their child. I'm getting out because I enjoy walking through my adopted neighborhood and interacting with people I see, not to mention that it's good exercise. Something that's forgotten amongst all of the bad news about child kidnappings, home invasions, and other crime on the streets is that the vast majority of people have no intention to do these things. In most places one is perfectly safe walking on the street regardless of the time of day.

While I'm in the vein of community and airing my grievances for a return to the values of the past, I'd also like to briefly touch on consumerism. Certainly this is a topic well worth mentioning in these economic times.

It's been tempered to an extent by the recessionary period of the last few years, but to many in our nation it's still all about our possessions, a mantra best expressed in the saying "he who dies with the most toys wins." And while I aspire like most others to be at least financially comfortable, to me it's more about life's experiences. There were points in my life where I could afford a larger house and more expensive car, but I knew that which I had was just fine and suited my purposes. I had more important goals in life to pursue, and even though they've changed over the years the sentiment still remains with me. If you read nothing else in this chapter, I want to make the point that, once the economy comes back, people need to spend less time and worry on acquiring stuff and more time on what's important, like being part of their community. Live within your means and outside your shell.

While I'm no financial expert, nor do I play one on TV, I suppose the best advice I can give to young people is to take the first 10% off your check and save that money someplace you can't easily touch it. Then pay your bills and groceries and such. Nor would it be a bad idea to cut up the credit cards – although shrinking home equity, long-term unemployment, and government interference have made it difficult to get them anyway.

Prior to the collapse of our financial markets, I would see and hear dozens of advertisements a week that tell the unsuspecting that they can have (and deserve) it all, just by simply refinancing your home. Never mind the deeper hole you dug for yourself just to take that cruise to Aruba or buy the big-screen TV you had to replace (with a bigger high-definition one, of course) in three years. You could deduct that home equity interest off your tax bill, but when the housing market went belly-up a lot of people lost everything they worked hard for because they were so overextended. We'll be having that financial hangover for many years to come, or at least until housing values rebound in, oh, maybe a decade?

In the last few years the "buy now, pay later" basis of our economy has taken a major hit. Still, smart people are able to land on their feet when adversity strikes. What has happened to the economic fortunes of those from the Baby Boom and Generation X serves as simple advice. It's up to my readers under the age of 30 to heed it and plan for the future wisely.

To that end, I'd love to see the next generation start to get away a little bit more from the Netflix or their Facebook page and get into other activities. Join a community organization, take part in a bowling league, even just take a walk around the neighborhood. If you have kids in school, get involved with their PTA. And believe it or not, my daughter's mom and I raised her in the 1990s without a television in her room, her own personal phone, or us having cable television. You can do this and turn out a child who becomes a productive adult. We've made mistakes along the way and so has she, but nothing too disastrous and we all learned from them. One mistake we made was wanting baubles we couldn't afford – luckily we worked our way through it.

I live in a nice area of somewhat older homes which aren't too expensive and were built back when craftsmanship wasn't a lost art. No, these homes aren't all really big and they're sort of close together, but I like it that way. And I think it's something we need to get back to.

The collapse of the real estate and mortgage sectors also work to reinforce my belief that people need to place a lot of thought into maybe not buying the largest, most expensive house that they can mortgage but instead purchase one that they can afford and turn into a home for the long run. Too many people have fallen prey to the allure of easy credit and have forsaken the old adage that anything good is worth working hard and saving for. Sometimes it takes a long time to attain the things in life that we all want, but it's more satisfying to have something and actually own it than it is to be mortgaged to the hilt.

I've dealt out a lot of advice in this chapter, so I'm going to close with a fond memory. My family once lived on a street of mostly older homes in a fairly middle-class neighborhood, ones which generally had those nice front porches overlooking the street. The most fun we had living there were the couple times where we as a group petitioned the city to temporarily close our street for an afternoon so we could hold a block party. One neighbor brought their cousin in to do a hog roast and the rest of us made up a potluck for the side items. It was a day the kids could run up and down the street without fear of traffic while the adults caught up with our neighbors and dodged the water balloons the kids were throwing at each other. Everyone ate well and we all chipped in a few bucks to pay for the hog roaster.

The event was a success because we had a good neighborhood where people got to know each other. And the neighbors who were the most enthusiastic about the idea were the ones who were older and raised in an era when being neighborly was valued, not having the nicest car or the biggest TV.

So this chapter is a call for community. Let's find ways to come together and by gosh have some fun with other people!

3

Property Rights and Eminent Domain

At one time in my life I was a member of the American Institute of Architects, with time spent in both the AIA Chesapeake Bay and Toledo chapters. Regardless of where I joined, politically the national song seemingly remained the same.

As a member I received the AIA e-mails at work, which I had zero problem with. It was good that the organization to which I paid dues kept me informed on what they were doing and those events where I may have wished to participate. But one of the e-mail missives I received was a newsletter called *The Angle*, which documented their political lobbying efforts and other related items the AIA pursued. A few years ago I got a newsletter soliciting input for a position statement, as follows:

Proposed Position Statement 46 - Eminent Domain

The American Institute of Architects believes that eminent domain is a critical tool for revitalizing our cities and improving the quality of life in urban and suburban neighborhoods. State and local governments must ensure that eminent domain laws do not curtail smart growth efforts, brownfield cleanup, or otherwise limit new development and improvements to existing development.

Well, since they asked for my input, they got it. My response:

I would feel much better about this if the statement read as follows:

"The American Institute of Architects believes that eminent domain is a critical tool for revitalizing our cities and improving

the quality of life in urban and suburban neighborhoods. While the AIA acknowledges and agrees that private property rights are paramount in our free society, we also feel that state and local governments can and should balance the rights of existing property holders with eminent domain laws that do not curtail smart growth efforts, brownfield cleanup, or otherwise limit new development and improvements to existing development."

As I read it, the AIA is taking a position of property holders be damned, we just want to develop sites regardless of who's hurt in the process and all these damn libertarians who insist on actually following the "takings clause" in the Fifth Amendment are just meddling with our profession.

Many eminent domain proceedings in the last decade have stretched the term "public use" way beyond its intent. Personally, I do not believe in government using its power and taking one's private property to benefit another person simply for additional tax revenue.

In this case, pressure from rank-and-file members and others interested did get to AIA to modify its position. It was a small victory, but a win nonetheless for those of us who still believe private property rights should be held sacrosanct.

It's pretty simple, really. The Fifth Amendment to the Constitution reads in part:

(N)or (shall a person) be deprived of life, liberty, or property, without due process of law; **nor shall private property be taken for public use, without just compensation**. (Emphasis mine.)

In 2005, the United States Supreme Court handed down what's known in shorthand as the *Kelo* decision (*Kelo v. City of New London.*) In a 5-4 decision (Justices Stevens, Kennedy, Souter, Ginsburg, and Breyer in the majority; Justices O'Connor, Rehnquist, Scalia and Thomas siding with Suzette Kelo) the Court upheld lower court rulings in finding for the city of New London,

Connecticut against aggrieved homeowner Suzette Kelo. Despite the fact *"the city (of New London) is not planning to open the condemned land – at least not in its entirety – to use by the general public,"* they noted, *"this…Court long ago rejected any literal requirement that condemned property be put into use for the… public."*

Sometimes the Supreme Court gets it wrong. The idea behind eminent domain was to allow the taking of private property for a public use, such as a highway, airport, or a building which would be owned by the taxpayers rather than a private entity. But in the case of Suzette Kelo, her property would have been used by a private developer who was planning on using the land to boost the city's tax base while profiting handsomely from using the government's eminent domain power – a textbook example of crony capitalism.

The bitter irony is that the development never got off the ground due to poor economic conditions and Pfizer (the drug manufacturer who envisioned the waterfront development as a boon to itself and the regional economy) abandoned the project in 2009, four years after getting its way in the nation's highest court.

The debate pointed out a loophole much used by cities that thought overall economic development was in the public's interest, regardless of who benefited. It's a similar argument to land issues when railroads were being built a century ago because railroads were owned by private interests but served the public good of transporting goods and passengers from town to town. In the modern-day case, the public good would be the creation of jobs and additional tax base for cities to compensate for services rendered to the whole population such as police and fire protection, trash pickup, and the like.

In the time since *Kelo*, several states have enacted or strengthened laws to prohibit the practice of government taking property from one private entity and granting it to another private entity for strictly economic reasons; a flurry of activity resulting in large part from the outcry caused by *Kelo*. According to one property rights advocacy group, the Castle Coalition, 42 states had either placed a prohibition on this practice or strengthened its position on the law by 2007, just two years after the Supreme Court spoke.

To use my adopted home state of Maryland as an example, the eminent domain power has not been used much in recent years for "traditional" items such as highways, airports, and government buildings. Here the heaviest user of eminent domain in recent years has been the Maryland Stadium Authority, as they cleared out blocks of homes and businesses to build, among others, Baltimore's M&T Bank Stadium (home of the NFL's Baltimore Ravens) and Oriole Park at Camden Yards. Many other cities and states have used similar tactics to build their sports facilities (along with millions of taxpayer dollars) in the hopes of creating economic development in the areas surrounding the stadium.

Much as I'm a sports fan, the idea of this chapter is not to argue the merits of cities like Minneapolis, Pittsburgh, Miami, and others building new facilities for their respective teams in their downtown area. These examples just happen to get more attention since they involve a sports franchise and its fan base in both the home city and around the country. Rather, my approach is to come up with a lasting solution which errs on the side of property rights.

Millions of Americans are invested in their homes and businesses. They made a bargain based on the fair exchange of their life's work, expressed in the money that changed hands, for real property. Thus, it shouldn't be a simple matter for these items to be taken away by government fiat without commensurate benefit to them. At times, the public good can and should take a back seat.

I like the idea of enacting a Constitutional Amendment at each state level, as some already have, as long as the amendment clearly states that the power of eminent domain is to be used only for the public good and not to enrich one powerful private entity at the expense of a caste of lesser entities as in Suzette Kelo's famous instance. Theoretically, the federal level is already taken care of by the takings clause in the Fifth Amendment; all that is required to maintain that protection is a Supreme Court which remembers our laws are based solely on what the Founders wrote, not what they feel is in our best interest at the time or excusing their decisions based on incorrect precedents.

Because this eminent domain issue has a fairly simple solution and can be settled rather quickly, it's one of the easiest planks to rectify in my manifesto. So I'm going to expand on the subject a little by talking in general about private property rights and the issue of growth. I touched a little bit on growth in my previous chapter on Community, and here again I look at the effects that overzealous activists have on our prosperity.

Obviously in our nation one has some restrictions on property rights, and generally they fall within the bounds of common sense. For example, it would not be a good idea to build a rifle range in the midst of a residential area. With utter and complete property rights a developer theoretically could plop down such an incompatible use, but most local areas have some sort of zoning to prevent these mishaps from occurring. Generally things like usage, setbacks, building area as a percentage of a lot, and building height are covered. These can also be waived if the property owner presents a compelling reason to do so in front of an elected or appointed local body.

However, I see a trend where government is restricting land usage by regulation. A recent example was embodied by the number of National Monuments established by President Clinton by his interpretation of the Antiquities Act of 1906. Whereas national parks are created through Congressional approval, in many cases national monuments needn't go through that process. Clinton established a total of 19 national monuments, mostly in the final year or so of his term. And while much of the land was already federally owned, this action further restricted its usage. By strokes of his pen President Clinton placed over 5 million acres of land out of reach to mining and development, an area about the size of New Jersey. More recently, the Omnibus Land Bill of 2009 signed by President Obama placed millions more acres out of reach to development.

While local zoning codes are generally fair because they have input from those most familiar to the issues faced by area residents, the scale of regulation of private property by the federal government is much less fair and much harder to combat. In particular, the federal government gets carried away in addressing the hypersensitivity by people concerned with environmental issues such as endangered species. A number of projects have been thwarted nationwide because so-called endangered species could – but did not necessarily – have a nesting ground or habitat on or around the site in question. While there's a case for preserving habitat, the balance is currently way too far in favor of militant environmentalism, at the expense of our economy.

Governmental entities should, in a perfect world, own the least amount of land necessary to function and to provide a suitable amount of recreational or scenic spaces for public use. But land which is owned by the government should also be as free of restrictions to private use as possible. While development would have limits, there are times where the public good outweighs the risks. One example is drilling for oil in the Arctic National Wildlife Refuge, a topic I'll address in a later chapter. With advances in both the exploration for and transport of crude oil, I think opening the refuge to exploration can be done if managed properly and carefully, but Congress has foolishly thought otherwise several times over the last decade.

Another incursion onto private property rights which doesn't stop at the walls of your home is coming from the "green" movement. Consider the advent in the last decade or so of the LEED-certified building.

LEED, which is an acronym for Leadership in Energy and Environmental Design, was created by an organization called the United States Green Building Council in the late 1990's to address how buildings could become more energy efficient and less taxing on the environment. The USGBC is one of those non-governmental organizations popular among the United Nations, one-world crowd.

Before I allowed the designation to lapse (because of program changes on the part of the USGBC) I passed the exam to become a LEED Accredited Professional, so I have a bit of a background in the field of "green" architecture. And while I'm a fan of making buildings more energy-efficient, I'm also mindful of the costs because in the end the job of a designer is to serve the clients' wishes insofar as they are practical when faced with a multitude of already-existing building and zoning codes.

Much of what LEED entails are common-sense measures to ensure energy efficiency - in fact, the system that LEED uses to determine whether buildings are simply Certified or meet the Silver, Gold, or Platinum plateaus also require construction to be energy-efficient enough to meet a national standard just to qualify for consideration.

Several municipalities, most states, and more recently the federal government are now mandating that their new institutional construction meet LEED certification standards, generally at least a Silver rating. For new buildings, this is equal to 50 of a possible 100 points (per LEED 2009 standards) granted for a variety of requirements in the areas of site selection, water efficiency, energy usage, and wisely choosing materials and resources for the job. However, there are also a number of prerequisites which must be met before the project would either be considered for certification by the USGBC or another standard deemed equivalent by the jurisdiction.

One LEED prerequisite in particular which troubles me is the prohibition on environmental tobacco smoke, or ETS.

While many of those governmental units who have adopted LEED standards derive a portion of their revenue from those who smoke cigarettes, the USGBC has undertaken to rid businesses of smokers. In order to meet a prerequisite to the Indoor Environmental Quality chapter, smoking is not to be allowed anywhere inside the building or within 25 feet of any possible air intakes such as entrances, operable windows, or intake vents. In residential cases, units have to be sealed thoroughly for air leakage while interior corridors are designed and tested for positive air pressure so smoke cannot filter through the building. All because some people find second-hand smoke offensive.

With the opening created by the LEED program, sympathetic government agencies are busy calculating other ways to control what you do in the privacy of your own home. For example, the state of California considered regulations which would require all newly built and renovated homes to have thermostats with a radio frequency receiver that would govern the setpoint temperature in the case of an "emergency." While the state later shelved the requirements, those Carter-era suggestions of keeping your thermostat at a chilly 65 degrees in the winter and sweltering 78 degrees in the summer may yet be enforced if the government figures out how to enact the measure more quietly in the name of fighting global climate change. One tactic seems to be that of "encouraging" utilities through making laws requiring them to offer these "smart meters" and remotely operable thermostats to customers in return for a bill credit. My local utility sends these offers to our household on a regular basis.

Let me be frank here. I'm of the opinion that mankind has practically nothing to do with global climate change. Before there were sport-utility vehicles the Vikings were growing grapes in Greenland (hence the name) and even with the warmer climate the ocean levels weren't significantly higher than they were now. Besides, who has determined that the climate we enjoy now is the optimal one anyway? I wouldn't mind more Florida-like winters here on the Eastern Shore of Maryland – especially after being blasted by snow measured in feet in the winter of 2010 and an abnormally chilly winter in 2011.

To me, much of the hype over climate change contributes to another front of the effort to usurp your right to do what you choose with what has become yours through sweat and toil. Locally determined zoning issues are one thing, but when some bureaucrat in your state capital, Washington or even the United Nations who has no idea about your situation decides that a drastic, one-size-fits-all solution is necessary, that force is much tougher to combat.

Changing these rules will take much longer to implement than the eminent domain issue will because, once again, it's going to take a sea change in attitude by the powers that be. The more land the government has and the more restrictions they place on usage of your own property, the more power they possess. It's going to take a constant and forceful voice from the people to make government at all levels give back to the private sector what is rightfully theirs.

Next, I'll transition from the right to own and use private property as one sees fit to the right we were given to defend it.

4

Second Amendment

In this era of "if it bleeds, it leads," the headlines regularly detail those who makes news for gunning down a whole host of people in a mass murder spree, with more ink devoted to those who assail a famous or prominent victim. As I wrapped up this book, the world heard the terrible news about the dozen people murdered in an Aurora, Colorado movie theater during a screening of "The Dark Knight Returns." Nearly sixty others were wounded, some critically.

Another fairly recent example was Jared Loughner, the gunman who allegedly shot Arizona Rep. Gabrielle Giffords in early 2011. While Rep. Giffords was lucky enough to survive the attack in front of a Safeway supermarket, six victims, including a nine-year-old girl, were not.

Four years earlier, in 2007, Seung-Hui Cho barricaded the doors of a Virginia Tech classroom and began firing indiscriminately, killing 32 people before turning the gun on himself.

The predictable knee-jerk reaction from the left in all these cases was, "we need more gun laws!" The sad fact is that no gun law would have prevented what happened. In each of these cases as well as thousands of others during the course of history, the gunman decided that his was the way to solve those personal problems he had, and people in the mindset to do damage to society will use whatever means they deem necessary.

The way I see it, the Second Amendment was placed in the Constitution because people having weapons would be able to protect themselves from a tyrannical government. Having broken away from a monarchy to establish what they hoped would be a truly republican government, the Founders worried about the reestablishment of oppression by a future society – thus, they decided that people should have the right to bear arms. It was "necessary to the security of a free state."

As states go, both Arizona and Virginia are among the least restrictive as far as acquiring a weapon – it's their perfect right to be so under the Tenth Amendment. Other states make citizens jump through hoops to get a gun, and that's also acceptable in the eyes of the Constitution. Meanwhile, accused Aurora gunman James Holmes reportedly acquired many of his accessory items, including ammunition, over the internet, adding another layer of complexity.

The main objection I have to the current situation, and the change that should guide policy in the coming decades, is working to eliminate federal gun laws. Just as the Constitution says, Congress shall make no law restricting the right we have to bear arms. However, pages and pages of the federal code deal with guns of all sorts.

I'm certain some will read this and think I'm trying to resurrect the wild, wild West. But my point is simple: laws that deal with guns (and a lot of other subjects too, guns just being the subject of this chapter) should be established by the individual states. If a state wants to disarm their populace, establish "gun-free zones" like the Virginia Tech campus or the Century 16 theater, and leave the weapons to the hands of the criminal element, well, that's their right. It would also be the right of the surviving public to throw those fools out of office who encouraged the situation by being a legislature full of gun grabbers.

On the other hand, states that show respect to their citizens by allowing them concealed carry and fewer restrictions on the number and type of guns they can possess are generally rewarded by lower crime rates. Imagine if even one person at these horrific crime scenes carried a weapon – there still would have been a number of deaths, but it may have been limited to the number the gunman could kill before someone else with a gun could have struck him down.

As I alluded to before, some say that the Second Amendment only covers people in a "well-regulated militia", a phrase they interpret as being in the National Guard or a like organization. However, the National Guard didn't come into being until the twentieth century. Nor is that the important part of the sentence, for the Second Amendment is sort of unique in that the militia language is descriptive rather than prohibitive. The amendment would have been just as effective without the militia portion of the sentence, simply reading "The right of the people to keep and bear arms, shall not be infringed."

It's also relative to a little-noticed and somewhat archaic portion of the Bill of Rights, the Third Amendment, which reads:

No Soldier shall, in time of peace be quartered in any house, without the consent of the Owner, nor in time of war, but in a manner to be prescribed by law.

Obviously the Founders reacted to the Crown's practice of quartering soldiers without permission. But by placing the two amendments consecutively, they wanted to stress that it was the people's right to both defend themselves against the government by allowing them to have weapons and to not have intrusion by agents of the government who carried weapons themselves and presumably would disarm the home's occupants, by force if necessary. This theme would carry through over the next several Amendments that addressed search and seizure, false prosecution, right to a speedy trial, and so on.

Federal gun laws weren't a significant impediment to the average person owning a gun until 1934, when the National Firearms Act was passed. That law was a reaction to the bootlegging and gang warfare which occurred during the Prohibition era. While that act placed little impediment on actually keeping weapons, it introduced the concept of registering guns. Gun laws were again tightened in 1968 with the passage of the Omnibus Crime Control and Safe Streets Act and the Gun Control Act. These measures passed in the wake of the assassination of two high-profile political figures, civil rights leader Dr. Martin Luther King Jr. and presidential candidate Robert F. Kennedy. Since then, both federal and state gun control measures have multiplied but crime statistics haven't appreciably dropped because of them. Rather, the trend has been for states which have less restrictive gun laws to see a corresponding decrease in criminal activity.

I've always subscribed to the theory that guns don't cause crime, people do. Someone with a gun has the ultimate ability to protect himself and his family – burglar alarms can be disabled and dogs can be killed or otherwise neutralized, but a gun in properly trained hands can be a deterrent even if it's not actually fired. Most criminals will think twice about tangling with an armed victim.

More importantly, an armed citizenry is more difficult for a government to control. One oft-repeated example is when Adolf Hitler consolidated his power in Nazi Germany, one of his first moves was to take away the guns from the citizenry. Without that basic protection, it was easier for Hitler to proceed with other sinister actions like the Final Solution. A general rule of despots and other thugs is that their citizens cannot be armed; that way it's much easier to control the public.

This is why we need to work the federal government out of gun regulation. The balance of power has gone so far away from law-abiding citizens and toward those who would prey on them that many big cities have large areas where only the foolhardy – or those who choose to ignore the gun laws – dare to go out at night.

I'm a supporter of people being able to keep whichever weapon they choose, but they also should be properly trained in how to use them. Just like people have to take a training course to drive an automobile, which can be a lethal weapon in the wrong hands, people should be trained on using and given an opportunity to gain respect for this powerful weapon. Once again, it goes along with my view that with rights come responsibilities.

But let's say I, a person who has no criminal record, want to buy a gun to protect myself. Postulating further, let's also say that I want to have the ability both to carry it where I wish and keep it concealed. In America today, there are so many hoops to jump through to not only purchase a gun but carry it where desired that I almost don't blame criminals for doing this illegally.

First of all, to buy a gun after my training I would need to go to a licensed firearms dealer. Not just anyone can sell me a gun legally, they have to go through the steps as a business to secure that license. Once I get there, they need to see my identification and in some instances I would need to have written permission from my local jurisdiction to purchase self-protection. They may also need to see proof I own a gun safe or I may need to simultaneously purchase a trigger lock.

Then I have a federal form to fill out, one that the dealer will keep on file. And if the dealer decides to go out of business, that form doesn't go away with the business – it becomes the possession of the federal government. Then comes the background check (also by the federal government) and a waiting period which varies from state to state.

So I've done all this and finally I get my gun. But getting to take it where I wish is another story. In order to be able to carry a concealed weapon, there's more paperwork to be filled out and permissions granted by either the state, the local jurisdiction, or both. There are various conditions which have to be strictly followed. But in this case, the federal government has by and large stayed out of the concealed carry arena. It would behoove states to work more toward a standardization and easing of these laws, placing more trust in the 99.99 percent of the citizenry who simply want to exert their right of self-protection.

I know many of those in law enforcement prefer stricter gun laws as it makes their job easier and less dangerous. A law enforcement officer dreads the domestic violence call when it comes in because their job is to go into an already volatile situation and attempt to defuse it without any of the parties being hurt. Adding a gun into the mix always puts lives in danger during those situations.

In these instances, it's up to the individual states to disallow ownership to certain people who have proven by their behavior that they cannot be trusted with the responsibility to own a weapon. Just like felons lose their right to vote in some places due to previous actions, it is not only the right of but the responsibility of a state (not the federal government) to deny some citizens gun ownership for a period of time in order to maintain public safety. These cases, though, should be few and far between.

While all of us need to work toward eliminating the onerous federal gun laws, we also need to make a goal of reestablishing a proper way of looking at crime and punishment in our country. In my next chapter, I'll take a look at why I think our conscience went away and how we can get it back.

5

Crime and the Justice System

Now that I've made the argument about reestablishing the proper Constitutional reach of the federal government in gun control, I'll shift gears a bit in this chapter and discuss on where I believe the justice system needs to readjust its focus.

In our justice system there are two separate types of cases: those on the criminal side and those on the civil side. There are problems with each but both have led to overcrowded court dockets.

Unfortunately, our legislative bodies continue to enact more and more regulations and ordinances, so the chances of you running afoul of a law increase. As an example, here in Maryland it became a law that a person may not catch oysters for sale without certifying they received information from the state about where oysters may not be harvested. So if you forget to send in this document, one of many pieces of paper the watermen in my area have to deal with, you would be in violation of the revised law. And obviously with more laws come more court cases. On the whole, it's likely readers of this book have knowingly or unknowingly violated dozens of local, state, and particularly federal laws today by just living their everyday lives.

I think the best way to solve this issue is to take a series of steps involving how we write laws and what we regulate. I'll begin with the federal level.

First of all, let's stop passing laws and regulations at the federal level mandating that states write some particular law or regulation on their part, penalizing them a portion of their federal funding for noncompliance. We've seen this with a variety of legislation, but the federal government is most notorious for playing this game with federal highway money. The funds are withheld if the individual states do not enact particular statutes the bureaucracy in Washington would like to see enforced. Through this carrot-and-stick approach, we've been saddled with mandatory seat belt laws, the raising of the legal age to consume alcohol to 21, and the lowering of the allowed blood alcohol level to .08 percent.

While many who read this book may say, "Michael, the examples you use are good common-sense rules for ensuring public safety," I agree these laws are noble for the most part and generally achieve their overall goal of enhancing public safety. But where does it stop? You may not have an objection to these particular laws I cited, but what mandate is next? Just in the arena of personal transportation alone, there are those who wish to curb the use of cell phones in cars through bans on texting and even hands-free operation, force motorcycle riders to wear helmets, or not allow smoking in cars in which children are riding. That's just one small portion of daily life.

All in all, to me the issue is a Constitutional one. The Tenth Amendment is there for a reason, so my message to you in Washington is to stop violating it. In fact, it's the impetus behind a small but growing Tenth Amendment movement spearheaded by TEA Partiers. They're known as "Tenthers" for their avid support of state's rights.

They support proposed laws being debated which assert states may reject what they consider onerous legislation, particularly as the federal government steps into the arena of health care with Obamacare. Along with the concept of nullification, where states choose not to enforce federal laws they feel are against the best interests of their citizens, over the last few years this movement toward states' rights, driven by pro-liberty forces, has taken root. Legislatures are finally listening to public demands that Washington bureaucrats be held in check and have formally bucked laws imposed by Washington regarding topics as diverse as medical marijuana, gun laws, and the Real ID Act.

While those of us with sound mind can work on eliminating the scam of holding back federal funding to the states, a concurrent step is for the states to junk many of the laws considered "nanny state" laws. Once again, these cover areas that properly fall under personal responsibility. To use one example I gave above, is it a crime that a driver doesn't wear a seat belt while driving or makes sure passengers are wearing theirs? I don't think so. I'll be the first to admit I do buckle up but to me that's a wise decision given the risk and I've made it my practice to use my safety belt even back before the law said I had to. But fearing the loss of that federal money, states knuckled under to Congress and enacted laws which made not wearing a seat belt a primary offense, one where you can be pulled over for that simple act of noncompliance. It's all part of a federal initiative called "Click It Or Ticket."

While I'm sure most states would probably maintain some sort of safety belt law without the mandate from Washington, a victory to me would be getting the primary offense aspect beaten back so police officers could better target more dangerous driving instead of pulling over a motorist who is only endangering his own self by not wearing the seat belt.

A place where reasonable suspicion could be better addressed is the fight against the scourge of gang activity in this nation. Once it was just the Crips and Bloods in East L.A. but now hundreds of groups are recognized by law enforcement nationwide as their own perpetrators of organized crime. States should allow the police more tools for enforcement and deterrence in situations where the First Amendment right "peaceably to assemble" is turning into a den of conspiracy – usually the gangs have subtle but obvious signs that they're colluding to cause trouble, whether the intent is physical violence, theft of property, vandalism, or the drug trade which provides the largest source of income for these illicit groups.

On a contrary note, I'm not sure that many of our drug laws regarding possession of small amounts are truly necessary – a number of states have taken the lead on becoming more lenient with medical marijuana than their federal cousins are. I can understand the idea of zero tolerance but it seems to have gone to a point where investigating and prosecuting the most minor offenses take up time that could be better spent on criminal organizations which profit from drug trafficking. Having a tiny amount of marijuana or growing a limited number of pot plants for personal use really shouldn't be a crime; however, the sale of it or driving under its influence should remain in the criminal realm.

In this case, I've not tried marijuana myself but have been in situations where it was smoked and offered to me. (That would be pretty much any concert I attended in my formative years, the 1980's.) So I guess I'm speaking as the anti-Clinton in that I didn't try it but I did inhale the second-hand smoke. On the whole, I equate growing marijuana for personal use with home brewing or wine making, both of which are legal in most locales.

If you haven't figured this out by now, my libertarian side is most pronounced when I discuss these sorts of issues. Of course I agree that there should be guard rails, but it should be the force of society shaming people into compliance rather than the force of law fattening government coffers and crowding our jails and prisons with drug offenders who were in most cases otherwise nonviolent.

While I'm on the side of not crowding our prisons with otherwise nonviolent drug offenders, I'd also like to see the prison populations reduced at the other end, death row. Those who have been proven beyond a shadow of a doubt with conclusive evidence that with malice and forethought they endeavored to end someone else's life should forfeit theirs. Unfortunately, endless legal appeals make the effort to carry out their punishment a costly one to the states so some have thrown up their hands, making a tacit decision not to follow through with executions. Just 13 states performed an execution in 2011, although only 15 states ban the practice. In most states, getting to the point of performing capital punishment is a cruel and unusual process requiring years in the courtroom and resulting only in justice delayed.

But without the death penalty as the ultimate punishment, a person who has it in their mind knows that they can get away with murder. They're aware that the worst society can do to them is lock them up for the rest of their life in a situation where escape is still possible. And even without escaping from prison, gang-related criminals have been known to order hits on the witnesses who placed them in confinement. They'd have a much more difficult time with this after assuming room temperature.

As a law-abiding citizen, I don't see that placing someone who brutally murdered another living soul in the electric chair as either cruel or unusual punishment, but instead as what they deserve. Yet there are those out there who feel that even the gentler method of execution many states use now, one where the condemned is basically put to sleep like your suffering family pet, is too cruel. To them I say: ask the families of those who died at the hands of the guilty about cruelty.

The other side of the legal system coin is the civil side. If you watch TV, drive down the road, or even look at your phone book, chances are sooner or later you'll see some lawyer advertising his or her services because you'll be screwed by the insurance company after your auto accident if you don't hire them, or else you should get what's "yours" because you took a particular prescription drug, was exposed to asbestos many years ago, or some other common real or imagined affliction – in other words, the class-action lawsuit.

And what has all this legal action gotten us? It's resulted in some extremely wealthy trial lawyers like two-time Presidential candidate John Edwards, who became rich on medical malpractice, or Baltimore Orioles owner Peter Angelos, who shook down companies making products with asbestos – and some extremely stupid warning labels placed on products because some idiot didn't use any common sense. However, he or she probably won life's lottery via class action lawsuit and added millions to a trial lawyer's bank account in the process.

While I don't begrudge anyone who works hard and puts in the hours of sweat and toil for their success – even the slimiest of trial lawyers – my thought is that just one measure is necessary to rid the system of a whole lot of junk lawsuits. It's called "loser pays." While the idea has floated around for a number of years, the idea maintains its validity and is probably more pressing than ever.

Of course, trial lawyers hate the idea, and so does the Democratic Party. They whine that "if you do 'loser pays' it will discourage the average citizen from filing a lawsuit." I counter that if their case has merit a good jury will hear their compelling evidence and decide in the plaintiff's favor.

Further, in many civil cases lawsuits reach a settlement long before they get to the courtroom because a company decides that it's better just to settle and make the problem go away at minimal cost than risk the prospect of John Edwards "channeling" an unborn child who ended up with cerebral palsy and swaying a jury with emotion rather than the facts behind the case. That doesn't necessarily go away with "loser pays" but trial lawyers will have to build up more airtight cases. (Hopefully the juries of tomorrow will also be better in critical thinking thanks to my ideas for education reform that I'll write about in Chapter 11.)

One idea that I've heard regarding trial by jury I don't care much for is the idea of paid professional jurors. Back in the day, people seemed to take jury duty more seriously than they do now – these days it's something to be avoided. You end up taking a day or more off work for the pittance that you're paid, a sum paid essentially to make up for the parking fee you're charged to keep your car at the courthouse all day.

So the idea was hatched about juror as occupation. While having professional jurors makes sense on some levels, I have to disagree with the concept as a whole because what you're doing in this case would be appointing more unelected judges – a panel of 12 professional arbitrators, if you will. Instead, being called for jury duty needs to be more mandatory, with fewer excuses for avoidance, but at the same time states and localities need to make it more lucrative with at least a minimum wage placed on it.

It's my contention that if "loser pays" is adopted, the result is that fewer trials will be clogging the courts, reducing the need for a jury pool, and the savings realized on that portion of the equation could be placed on making jury duty less of a financial hit to the people who are asked to perform this public service our Founding Fathers incorporated into the Sixth Amendment.

Our system of justice has worked pretty well for over 200 years. But the courtroom should not be a place where a trial lawyer strikes gold by playing to the emotions of twelve jurors in order to convince them that, hey, this company won't miss the $30 million I'm seeking to have awarded to my client (never mind I'll get a large percentage of the settlement); nor should it be the place where one who is growing marijuana solely for personal use ends up risking a jail term.

To conclude this chapter I have one more point. Quite simply, I think regulations and many laws should have a sunset date. As one example, the PATRIOT Act was set up originally to expire in four years; however, many in Congress thought that it should become permanent because terrorism could be a recurring threat for the foreseeable future. But where a lessening of civil rights is concerned, any measure curtailing them should be temporary. I think a ten year sunset period on laws is a good time frame; first, it allows a legislative body which has turned over to some degree with new members to revisit the law and its consequences; and secondly, if they're looking at existing laws it's less likely they'll think of new ones!

Many existing laws which need to be revisited have to do with the issue of life, particularly in the case of abortion. My next chapter deals with that and other areas where we need to restore the culture of life.

6

Life

There are two elements to this thing I'm calling life. One is the beginning and how it's been affected by the court system over the last forty years. The other side is what happens as life approaches its end.

Regarding this topic, Americans tend to fall into two groups whose aims are similar but who believe in different means to get what they desire. There are some who believe legislating morality is a place for government – even as they would welcome an overall reduction of government's role – while others would prefer that Big Brother butt out of their bedrooms. That second group, however, also has a subset that makes it clear they believe with rights come responsibilities which fall on the shoulders of individual citizens, not government. Many on all sides have participated in debates over these issues over the years, and while the goals of those citizens who are most politically active on the conservative front tend to be fiscal in nature, there is a strong streak of social issue awareness running though the group as well.

Over the next several decades all of us will deal with issues at both ends of the life cycle as new children are created and those of us already here continue along the path toward old age. In particular, we're going to see an unprecedented graying of America as the millions of Baby Boomers born between 1946 and 1963 approach an age where their progeny will be forced to care for them financially, directly as caregivers, or in many cases both.

It was a Baby Boomer who made abortion a contentious issue in this nation. Born in 1947, Norma McCorvey was the plaintiff in *Roe v. Wade*, a case where the Supreme Court established that women have the right to secure an abortion within certain parameters. By reading between the lines of their apparently living, breathing Constitution, the Supreme Court established a woman's right to privacy and opened the door to terminating pregnancy for convenience. More importantly, they wrested the process of enacting abortion restrictions from the individual states.

Tens of millions of abortions later, the issue remains a hot-button one for thousands of activists on both sides. While groups like the National Organization for Women and NARAL Pro-Choice America wish to keep abortion legal (but supposedly rare), religious groups generally line up on the pro-life side of the issue, with many proposing a Human Life Amendment (HLA) to the U.S. Constitution.

While I think the HLA idea is admirable, there are two problems with the approach sought by the pro-life community. First of all, there's the daunting hurdle of getting the amendment through Congress. With a 2/3 supermajority required in each house of Congress, there's little chance in the near future that enough in the House or moreso the Senate would line up behind an amendment guaranteed to provoke the ire of the radical feminist movement. While time has shrunk the numbers of those feminists who Rush Limbaugh calls "feminazis" because they want as many abortions as possible, they maintain control of significant financial resources and in this day and age of politics inside the Beltway, money talks. (A sad commentary to be sure.)

An even larger problem is that a small minority of thirteen states can derail the process. While the roadblock of getting the support of the 2/3 of each house of Congress required to enact a Constitutional amendment is severe, having to convince the 3/4 of states required for passage on the merits of ratifying any such change against the powerful pro-choice lobby makes it all but impossible. The Founders made it hard to amend the Constitution intentionally so that much time and debate would be required to make changes in the fundamental law of the land. Moreover, it only takes five judges on the Supreme Court to render any portion of the Constitution useless by reading things into it which aren't there (like a right to privacy) or ignoring items spelled out clearly.

Thus, for the last forty years pro-life forces have been fighting an uphill battle despite the fact that a majority of Americans agree that restrictions on abortion are necessary. But I think the next two generations can provide the tipping point to restoring the right to life in America that dates all the way back to the Declaration of Independence.

The first step, though, can be provided by a President who is willing to appoint judges who read the Constitution as written. At some point in the fight to restore a life-affirming culture *Roe v. Wade* has to be vacated as a decision and precedent, so we need jurists who aren't afraid to abandon the Supreme Court's guiding principle of *stare decisis* when precedent is at odds with what the Founders intended. While the topic was unrelated to abortion, the Roberts Court corrected a century of incorrect precedent in the 2010 *Citizens United v. FEC* case by throwing out ill-advised campaign finance laws, so the time may soon be right to revisit *Roe v. Wade* – if intelligent jurists are indeed found.

Another parallel track in the process would be taking the fight to the states, asking them to enact their own versions of the Human Life Amendment. Among other things, a state-level HLA can provide protection to the unborn in states which don't want to depend on their more liberal brethren to ratify a Constitutional amendment by establishing that life begins at conception, at least within their borders.

While I identify quite a bit with libertarians on a number of issues, I part ways with those who believe that it should be the woman's choice to terminate her pregnancy because she has ownership of her body. Since they further surmise a fetus cannot survive outside the womb, they don't consider the unborn as someone who's gained the right to life and liberty.

I have two counter-arguments to their contentions. First of all, we're also forgetting that there is another person who was involved in the creation of the child. While perhaps he (and/or she) took steps to prevent the pregnancy from occurring, the fact remains that they created another living being. If they don't want to raise the child, there are thousands of couples out there who desperately want to have a child but cannot for various biological reasons.

Secondly, what definitive artificial point can be established that measures whether a fetus is viable? In the last few decades, we've brought the point where a baby born prematurely can survive back to around 24 weeks after conception. Moreover, there may come a day when the technology will be there for artificial wombs and the like, not to mention human cloning and other alternative reproductive methods. In those cases, where can personhood start other than at conception?

But back to the HLA. By taking the case directly to state legislative bodies, activists maintain the concept of states' rights and bring the issue closer to the people. Yes, the approach may provide a checkerboard pattern of states providing complete abortion access astride states with prohibitions, but this is probably the best way the pro-life movement can achieve its aim when it comes to curbing the practice of abortion. Instilling a culture of life may become more and more important as advances in neonatal technology not only allow the sex of a baby to be determined but eventually other genetic characteristics such as being prone to certain diseases. It's also possible the nullification of *Roe v. Wade* by a state HLA, with its corresponding restrictions on abortion, could eventually become the court case that gets *Roe* overturned.

Yet there is one other cultural aspect which needs to change, and I think the lack of respect for the culture of life stems back to this particular factor.

Back when my generation was kids there were a vast number of hazards we were exposed to. Parents today, though, recoil in horror if they learn their children have to endure the same things.

For starters, my peers grew up with plenty of exposure to lead. Back them one could purchase paint filled with the stuff, as too was the gasoline our smog-belching cars burned and emitted. (I'm sure some who read this book and disagree with my assertions may suspect I was exposed to more than my share of lead from these and other point sources.) And those cars didn't have three-point safety belts nor were child seats commonly available. My two brothers and I had free, unshackled reign in the back seat of our 1969 Plymouth.

Then when school was out for the summer we'd go out early in the morning on our bikes – without a helmet – and play pickup four-on-four baseball on the sandlot under the blazing summer sun without any sort of protective gear. Of course we chose sides and kept score in these games, meaning we were out to win – so some kids like me were picked toward the end because we just weren't as talented as the more athletic kids. For those frequent arguments during the game, we had our idea of conflict resolution called the do-over. But sometimes things eventually had to be settled another way and somebody would end up with a black eye or bloodied lip.

Most importantly, when we screwed up badly and our parents found out, there wasn't a "time-out." Instead there was generally a stern lecture on what we did wrong, but that came only after the swat or two on the behind to reinforce the point that was about to be made.

The point is our parents were parents who let us be kids and most of us still grew up to be productive adults. Once in awhile, we would get hurt – our arms, our knees, our feelings – but we made it through.

Fast forward to the present day where we have kids whose lives are completely regimented by a number of activities. Maybe that's why when it comes to parenting the kids of my generation really dropped the ball. Certainly there are more predators out there, as one unfortunate by-product of the society we live in is that we have to put up with these animals; still, nowadays children are protected from being kids by an effort to wipe away all possible risk of harming themselves.

Yet the right sort of protection doesn't come from using a bike helmet or playing baseball with a Nerf bat. I'm a firm believer that having a caring stay-at-home parent can be a huge advantage in raising a child that grows up to respect other people and life in general. Later in this book, I make the argument that policies can be enacted to make it easier for parents to have the opportunity to be home with their children.

Otherwise, parents may have to reap what they sow later in life. Children who are ignored by their parents tend to arrive at the conclusion that, after their parents become an inconvenience in their later years, they can be done away with. Just like the question of fetus viability, who determines the point where life is no longer worth living? Some people have living wills which provide a guide to their final wishes, but most parents don't think about these things when they're still of sound mind and body to do so and leave it up to their children to decide. Keep in mind that Boomers like Norma McCorvey are now much closer to being the subject of end-of-life issues than their childbearing years.

Euthanasia didn't become a national issue until a couple decades back when Dr. Jack Kevorkian performed the first of what would become dozens of assisted suicides, generally carrying out the wishes of chronically to terminally ill patients to die peacefully and painlessly. He evoked a great deal of sympathy for his cause but also served a lengthy prison term in Michigan for carrying out what the state considered to be murder. The right-to-die movement became prominent thanks to the man some called "Jack the Dripper."

Some equate the act of assisted suicide to putting a family pet to sleep once a veterinarian has determined that the animal has a disease or chronic painful condition without a hope for a cure. But the difference to me is that an animal doesn't have a cognitive survival instinct beyond a simple "fight or flight" mentality, whereas humans can and sometimes do make the decision to end their own lives despite our own survival instinct. Fido doesn't know it has a disease that will shortly and painfully end its life and wouldn't have the decision-making skill to know that running out in front of a bus would bring a quick termination, but Fido's owner understands this and doesn't want to see the animal suffer. In many cases, human beings are aware of the circumstances they are or soon will be in – witness Ronald Reagan's memorable "I now begin the journey that will lead me into the sunset of my life" announcement about the Alzheimer's Disease that eventually ended his life – but there are times where events dictate the person gets no say in the matter of life or death.

For over fifteen years, Terri Schiavo lay suspended between life and death as the battle between her husband and her parents raged in the courts whether to continue extraordinary measures to keep her alive or allow her to starve to death. Part of the controversy arose from the cause of her affliction, which was suspicious, but the main argument came from Michael Schiavo's assertion that Terri wouldn't want to live in her persistent vegetative state.

The debate raged through the Florida court system and even to the halls of Congress before Michael Schiavo finally won and Terri Schiavo was allowed to die in 2005. It was a case which placed the pro-life and pro-states' rights wings of the conservative movement at odds with each other.

I feel that we should err on the side of preserving life, and the Schiavo case proved there's still an intact culture of life in this country. On the other hand, some in the federal government tried to go too far with measures which stepped on Florida's right to make its own laws. It's the charge of coming generations to encourage states to adopt rules which err on the side of preserving life in cases like Schiavo's and have judges that respect laws which are made through due process, in accordance with the state and federal Constitutions.

While the right to life is front and center on our Declaration of Independence, it deserves more respect than it's seen over the last few years. And not only have some infringed on thatright of existence, there are those who believe the government should play a bigger role in how you live yours. My next chapter begins a look at the mess our entitlement system is in and what can be done to address it.

7

Role of Government

This chapter, along with Chapter 8 on fiscal responsibility, will work to set the table for later chapters. With those I'll look at some of the many entitlements our federal government has eased into over the last several decades.

Each January, the President follows his Constitutional mandate and delivers the State of the Union address. Since I'm generally out enjoying life I don't actually watch the speech but read it online after it's delivered. This takes me about 5 minutes, thus saving me about an hour of my life. In most years that's about the only savings I see out of it.

For years Presidents of both parties have used the SOTU speech as a showcase for whatever programs they wanted to push. Invariably, these were billed as panaceas for problems that faced our nation, and always it was a Federal solution that would cure the ailment. All these new programs seemingly either created or extended Federal mandates on what states or private enterprise may do.

What isn't delivered during the address are the unintended consequences of promises that are made. As my favorite example of many where recent events have given us the opportunity to measure the impact of unintended consequences I give you the Corporate Average Fuel Economy standards; better known as CAFE. In his 2007 State of the Union presentation, President George W. Bush called for increasing these standards and got his wish later that year with the passage of the Energy Independence and Security Act of 2007.

Even setting aside the GM and Chrysler bailouts, there's no question the automotive industry has seen its share of turmoil in the four years since that declaration. The surge in gas prices to $4 a gallon during the summer of 2008 did more to decimate the large sport-utility market than the future changes in the CAFE regulations did. Increasing the tempo of change to CAFE standards, as has occurred under President Obama, will make more and more large gas-guzzling vehicles of all sorts a thing of the past.

Yet in recent years, even when gas prices were relatively steep, the automotive market had favored large sport utility vehicles which came in below average on the fuel efficiency chart. While they didn't pass by very many service stations, these units provided the largest profit margins for the Big Three automakers.

Even though gasoline prices have retreated from the price spikes of 2008 and 2011, raising CAFE standards may well mean less profit for the Big Three because they can't sell as many of the roomy cars and trucks favored by the market regardless of gasoline prices. Michigan's economy was already hurting as the Big Three teetered on the edge of bankruptcy before Uncle Sam bailed out the United Auto Workers and gave them partial ownership of GM and Chrysler, and raising the CAFE standards will eventually be another blow to their efforts at recovery. Moreover, the Wolverine State is still slow to recover from the Great Recession despite all federal efforts at assistance.

Some may argue that continuing to update the standards would force the automakers to design and sell cars and trucks which are more fuel-efficient, and indeed that has been the case. They've had to phase out the large behemoths – GM's Hummer nameplate and the massive Ford Excursion SUV being just two of the casualties – and figure out ways to make cars lighter and more aerodynamic. But safety is also a factor as basic physics shows that smaller, lighter objects fare more poorly in accidents. Eventually that would lead to more highway fatalities, which would create a call for more safety equipment, which in turn makes cars that much heavier and less fuel-efficient. And the cycle would continue, as it has over the last five decades of evolving regulations where we oscillate between encouraging safety and the thrifty use of gasoline.

The cycle is accelerating even faster as I write this book, with President Obama enacting not just accelerated CAFE standards, mandating a fleetwide average of nearly 60 miles per gallon, but also approving government investment in renewable fuels and advanced battery technology for automotive transport, among other energy-related items. I'm all for innovation and making products better, but I believe we should let the market dictate what eventually succeeds, not the government. The Obama administration is still being stung by instances where they certainly didn't pick the "sure bet" such as Solyndra, the green job fiasco where taxpayer money which provided loan guarantees to the bankrupt solar panel maker – to the tune of over $500 million – is likely unrecoverable.

This green energy example is one of many which falls into a category that has bothered me for as long as I've been a student of politics. It's the basis of this chapter on the role of government.

I keep a small booklet-sized copy of the Declaration of Independence and Constitution on my desk. The Tenth Amendment reads:

The powers not delegated to the United States by the Constitution, nor prohibited by it to the States, are reserved to the States respectively, or to the people.

The first and foremost objection I have to the current method of government (practiced by both parties; neither is blameless in this) is when Congress puts together a bill that holds either the carrot of giving additional Federal funds or the stick of a Federal money cutoff to a particular state based on their action or inaction on a particular measure. I touched on this on Chapter 5, but one example I see as I drive into Maryland is the sign stating that .08 blood alcohol level is the law here. Apparently Maryland was one of the last states to lower the allowable BAL to .08 from the previous .10 but got with the program once their highway funding was threatened.

One of my former Senators was responsible for this. While he was in Congress, former Senator Mike DeWine of Ohio tragically lost one of his daughters to a car accident involving a drunk driver. But if he had been a proper government servant he would have lobbied the state of Ohio to lower its BAL limit as part of a statewide effort to promote highway safety. Instead, after trying for several years to get this adopted, he managed to place this stick in other Congressional legislation. Thereafter, states like Maryland eventually knuckled under to the threat of losing part of their federal highway funding if they didn't follow the lower BAL standard.

My neighbors to the north in Delaware also face this for not having a federally-compliant open container law. Because they're non-compliant, each year the state has a small percentage of its federal highway funding "diverted" to a federal program to combat drunk driving. Of course, that makes me wonder whether they'll ever get a bonus from all the years money was withheld if they ever get into full compliance. I doubt it!

Yet again, it's an example of the stick being applied to a state government to bend over to the wishes of the federal government, which is once again overreaching its Tenth Amendment rights.

When you add in all of the programs in the laundry list that the State of the Union address is known for advocating, it's highly likely that state and local governments will continue to be placed at the beck and call of what some bureaucrats and do-gooders in Congress want them to do. If you give health insurance to your heretofore uninsured residents, we'll give you more money. If you don't enact the federal No Child Left Behind regulations, we'll take away your federal education funding. (The same principle applies to taxation for individuals as certain actions are either encouraged or discouraged, but that's a topic for Chapter 13.)

There are three principles I'd like to see those who are supported by TEA Partiers and other conservatives embrace when they get to positions of power.

First and foremost is an end to these government mandates. Let the states comply with the old saw about being individual laboratories of government. It's a shame that all the faceless bureaucrats who get to push paper and make sure that the lower reaches of government do exactly as they have dictated to them would lose their jobs, but perhaps their talents can be used effectively in some other task – like digging ditches. Lord knows eliminating red tape would open up a lot of jobs in the private sector!

The second principle is not something that the Founders intended, but I've come to believe in the last few years they've become necessary. Additionally, the Constitution now has a precedent for it in the 22nd Amendment and it's a favorite topic for debate among those who believe in limited government.

At one time I subscribed to a fairly libertarian theory that term limits were bad policy because you deny voters all of the possible choices for a particular office, and they just may like having a career politician represent them. But over the last few years, as I've seen hundreds of politicians seek term after term and spend decades in office, I've changed my thinking.

Our Founding Fathers intended political duty as something done for just a few years, which is why the House of Representatives was set up to be elected by the people every two years. Many don't realize that the Senate was set up with six year terms in part because Senators were not directly elected by the people, but originally chosen by each state's legislature. The longer terms were in order to bring continuity to the office when there was turnover in state legislatures on a regular basis. These term lengths were not changed when the Seventeenth Amendment was ratified in 1913; as the Constitutional change only altered the method of selecting Senators. Meanwhile, the amendment dealt a blow to states' rights by eliminating their representation at the federal level.

While term limits may seen an unnatural limit on the will of the people, the principle is already in the Constitution as the 22nd Amendment. Ratified in 1951, it codified what had been a long-standing tradition of not running for a third presidential term started by George Washington and carrying through until Franklin Roosevelt defied the norm by running for a third term in 1940. Prior to FDR, no President had served more than two terms. Teddy Roosevelt ran for what would've been almost a third full term in 1912, as he was elevated from Vice-President upon the assassination of President McKinley in 1901, but he had been out of office since 1909 so the terms would not have been consecutive.

Further, since the Amendment was ratified, regular change has occurred at the executive branch. A party holding the office of President for 8 years has been the norm over the last half-century, except for the years of Jimmy Carter through George H.W. Bush. Democrats only held the presidency for one term under Carter (1977-81) before the GOP held sway for 12 years (1981-1993, Reagan and G.H.W. Bush.) We returned to an eight year cycle with Bill Clinton and the trend continued as the Republican George W. Bush was succeeded by the Democrat Barack Obama after serving eight years.

But this change does not occur in lesser levels of government. A number of Congressmen and Senators, generally Democrats who favor an all-encompassing government, have held their offices 30 years or more. Once entrenched, they become obstacles to reform. For example, the Congressional district I grew up in (Ohio's Ninth) has had the same Congressman since 1983. She was one term removed from another entrenched Democrat veteran who held the seat for 26 years.

Nor are Republicans immune: the adjacent district (Ohio's Fifth) was home to one GOP Congressman who held the office for 30 years before retiring. His successor held the seat for another eighteen before dying in office, only to be succeeded by the son of the original officeholder.

I think there needs to be a Constitutional amendment for term limits for Congress; in this session both Senator Jim DeMint of South Carolina and Rep. David Schweikert of Arizona have introduced such a proposal.

The same is true in the Senate. Looking at my adopted home state's representation there, Maryland has one Senator who has held her seat since 1987, with the other recently beginning his Senate career after two decades in the House of Representatives. In turn, he took over for a Senator who served 30 years. But none of these illustrious members of Congress hold a candle to those who have (or had until recently) served in their offices since the Eisenhower Administration - Congressman John Dingell of Michigan and the late Senator Robert Byrd of West Virginia.

The Founders intended a legislature composed of public-minded citizens who would serve a short time in Congress then return home to their communities. As noted before, President George Washington embodied this principle by refusing to serve a third term despite the fact he would've almost certainly won in a landslide.

Because Congress won't make a move toward term limits, we need to look at how the states handle the question. One state which has adopted term limits is Ohio, which through a popular vote enacted eight-year term limits for its state officeholders. But their law, like that of many other states, has a serious weakness. What's happened in a few cases is that legislators who run through their four (two-year) terms in the Ohio House run for the Ohio Senate to take advantage of its eight-year limit (two four-year terms) and *vice versa,* then come back to run for the House again once that eight years is up. Without a lifetime limit, there's no incentive for career politicians in the state to return to private life. Not only that, legislators in Ohio have also considered lengthening the limits to twelve years, so the law of my native state is no model to adopt.

Instead, to combat the idea of switching back and forth every few terms, I'd also like added to the federal law a lifetime limit of 24 years in Congress (six terms in the House plus two terms as Senator.) States should also consider, as a handful have, lifetime limits in their legislatures too.

As I pointed out earlier, one argument against term limits is that they artificially limit the voter's right to choose their representative

– if they want Congressman X to run and win his twentieth term, by God that should be their right. Well, I would have liked another term for Ronald Reagan while others may have wanted Bill Clinton to maintain his residence in the White House. Since we've already lost that right to do so with the President through the 22nd Amendment, being consistent dictates we do the same with the legislative branch.

A second argument postulated against the concept of term limits is that a legislative body suffers the loss of institutional leadership, especially if it's adopted at the federal level and we see the first wave of Congressmen and Senators reach their twelve-year limit. What of seniority, they ask? And how about those entrenched bureaucrats and lobbyists who would take control since they don't have to stand for re-election?

I'll answer the second question first by reminding readers that a limit to mandates puts many of these bureaucrats out of work, returning them to jobs where they actually have to produce things of tangible value as opposed to gobbledygook. As for the charge about institutional memory, my answer is that the bodies in Congress operate by a set of rules that most of those who possess the intelligence required to win and occupy the seat in the first place should be able to comprehend in the first few weeks of their term. And having regular turnover goes hand-in-glove with the third principle I favor; one which may be the most controversial.

The third leg of a limited-government stool that I'd like to see adopted is the automatic sunsetting of government rules and regulations after a point in time, say, ten years. Just as many government programs need to be reauthorized from time to time, like No Child Left Behind for federal education standards or the State Childrens' Health Insurance Program (better known as SCHIP), I contend that encoded laws and (particularly) regulations themselves need to be revisited occasionally.

After the 9/11 attacks Congress enacted the PATRIOT Act, which curbed some of the civil liberties that libertarians in particular hold dear. The original authorization was for three years so it had to be passed anew by Congress in 2005 – meanwhile, some of the PATRIOT Act's rabid supporters called for the provisions to become permanent.

I understand how curbs on certain rights may be required during a time of war. During the Civil War, President Lincoln suspended the right of *habeas corpus* for a short time as part of prosecuting the war. President Franklin Roosevelt interred thousands of Japanese-Americans during World War II. In neither case was there much debate about these actions by Congress, as the Executive deemed these actions necessary for prosecution of the war.

But to me the PATRIOT Act provisions need not become permanent, as at some point in our future the Long War against Islamic-based terrorism will be won. (If it's not, then the diminished rights we enjoy now would become meaningless. I don't think there's a right of *habeas corpus* in Shari'a law.) By keeping the regulations as closed-ended, it makes them easier to remove once the threat no longer exists.

As a further argument for sunsetting, many have made a living poking fun at some archaic law which has long since outlived its usefulness but still languishes on the books. While these rules may have been placed originally for noble purposes, the fact is these old regulations are still enforceable and could be abused for the simple purpose of harassing a particular person or group. My idea makes certain the law books have a good pruning on a regular basis.

Moreover, if a Congress is debating the merits of existing laws that have come to the end of their sunsetting period, they have less time to dream up new restrictions! And if the term limit principles I've touched on earlier were simultaneously adopted, it would be an almost entirely new Congress which debates the issue and they wouldn't have the ownership aspect to color their view. To use one example, would John McCain (now in his mid-seventies and a Senator since 1987) or Russ Feingold (who occupied his Senate seat for three terms) have been in favor of repealing their campaign finance law? Doubtful, but if it came up for renewal in ten years their successors may feel differently.

In my thinking about the role of government, I believe I have envisioned something a little closer to what the Founders intended. As it stands right now, the governmental pyramids are inverted – power is concentrated at the top, but that's where the fewest people wield it. I believe government was intended to have the maximum power placed at the bottom of the pyramid with the people, then the "several States" above them, with the federal government at the peak of the pyramid, occupying a perch where they were only intended to do things in the national interest like coining money, foreign relations, and defending our nation. The Constitution addressed the failings of the original Articles of Confederation and defined the roles of government more clearly.

As I stated when I began this book, this change is not one that's going to happen overnight – it's going to take decades and the generation of my daughter and whatever children she's blessed with to accomplish these goals. But I believe it's possible and it just may refresh the tree of liberty without shedding the blood of patriots, tyrants, or bystanders.

Once the role of government is more clearly defined and brought closer to the people, it will be easier to restore the power of the purse to where it rightfully belongs. I look at that in my next chapter.

8

Fiscal Responsibility

It's not just sheer happenstance that I write this chapter at a time when budget battles are looming at all levels of government. Pick any city or county in America and chances are you'll find the locals fighting over some sort of tax or spending increase – usually both at the same time. Meanwhile the state government the local jurisdiction depends so much on to supplement their local tax dollars is looking to combat their own structural deficit of some kind. Of course, dictating the entire dance is the federal government, a group that has placed itself in the position of holding everyone's purse strings while making a show of trying to whittle down its deficit spending; well, at least once in awhile they do. Sometimes they believe (wrongfully) that deficit spending is advantageous for the economy.

Over the last few decades a number of ideas have been bandied about as possible solutions to the problem of government overspending, most notably at the hog trough that is Washington, D.C. In this chapter I'm going to talk about three of these in particular. Furthermore, I'm going to state my case that the government's ongoing attempts at economic "stimulus" and passing "jobs bills" are not only short-sighted but dangerous to our long-term fiscal well-being.

As a place to begin, many have attempted to jump-start the process of streamlining Washington by introducing a balanced budget amendment to the Constitution. Their argument goes that most states have a balanced budget amendment so the federal government should as well.

There are times I would agree with that; however, in this era of an open-ended war with the forces of radical Islam, a balanced budget may not be readily attainable. Usually a balanced budget amendment leaves an exemption for times of war, and, whereas states cannot declare war, the federal government retains the right to do so. Also, since 2001 the government has a stated position of dealing with the national security threat brought about by radical Islamists and their allies globally in any and all ways possible. It's only the methods of practice that differ.

Given this national security threat a balanced budget amendment is probably not in the cards, at least for the foreseeable future. After all, for several years we had a Congress which made a great show of passing "PAYGO" bills where – in theory – additional government spending was offset by either cuts to other programs or by revenue enhancements (read: higher taxes.) In one case, Congress couldn't even make it two weeks without violating PAYGO in order to pass a "jobs bill."

But there is one rarely mentioned solution that's very simple to adopt. All we need is legislation to end the federal practice of "baseline" budgeting.

Reading this book you may ask, "what is baseline budgeting?" Let me illustrate the concept.

Imagine you're looking at your yearly budget. You have a mortgage payment, utilities, expenses for your car, groceries to buy, an amount for new clothing, and so forth. In looking at the budget you used the year before you say to yourself that as a rule you're going to assume you'll spend 10 percent more this year on all of these items. Unfortunately, once you start down that path sooner or later you'll see that unless your income went up 10 percent to match those expenditures, things don't work in your budget and you must make a few spending cuts. (Not to mention in this economy you're lucky if you're not staring at a 10 percent cut in your income, assuming you still have a job. If you're not looking at a decrease in income, then you must work for the federal government!)

In the case of the federal government their bean counters automatically assume these increases will take place when they calculate the federal budget. (I won't even take a peek at all the off-budget expenses for fear of making your head explode.) By using this practice they've developed a great defense mechanism for those who favor expanding government because now even a smaller increase in the rate of spending is defined as a spending "cut." Using this perverse version of new math, if a 10 percent increase is set as the baseline, an increase of only 8 percent becomes defined as a 2 percent budget cut.

And because the federal government has no restriction on deficit spending, they don't have any incentive to tighten their belt like many states and certainly the rest of us do when income doesn't equal outgo. But by ending the baseline budgeting practice, the result would be more truthfulness in the budgetary process, and a 10 percent spending increase in real dollars gets reported as just that. Having that information just might beg the question why such a large increase is deserved by the governmental agency or department.

To me, it's no coincidence that these budgetary rules, enacted way back in 1974, parallel an era where practically every federal budget has been awash in a sea of red ink. Only the strong efforts at welfare reform and cutting other entitlements by the Gingrich-led Republican Congress in the late 1990's netted a small budgetary surplus during the period; even so the national debt continued to swell because of the usage of Social Security money as an asset – another budgetary trick I'll discuss in the upcoming chapter on that program.

Once the die is cast and real numbers showing budget increases or cuts become the yardstick by which the federal budget is determined, government can take further steps to clean up the process of "earmarks" for good. Here the states have a role to play as well.

Not too many years ago I was at a local party meeting where we had our former state Senator, a good fiscal conservative, as a guest speaker. Naturally the subject of state spending came up for discussion and this well-respected voice in the Maryland Senate made a clear statement on the issue.

What the esteemed Senator brought up is a common problem. Like most other states, Maryland has a capital improvements budget featuring what are known locally as "bond bills." Also similarly, what occurs during the portion of Maryland's General Assembly session devoted to the budget is a lot of serious horse-trading and competition for an amount which, quite honestly, can be defined as budgetary scraps (perhaps $20 million out of a $35 billion state budget) as legislators scramble to secure pork for their districts.

The point the Senator brought up was that you have two choices: one of which is taking the high road and not seeking any money for the district as a means of cutting spending. Unfortunately, there's always another legislator without those scruples who would be happy to fund something in his or her district to use that money for since it's going to be made available anyway. The other unpleasant alternative is where you can sort of hold your nose and grab for as much cash as you can get, which indeed is distasteful but reflects the sad reality that the money is going to be made available because practically all legislators enjoy being in power and do their hardest work in the area of passing out pork to assure reelection. Yes, I call it buying votes.

Now multiply that by the other 49 states plus 50 states' worth of elected officials on the federal level and you see why our financial house is so far out of order – especially when there's a theoretically limitless money supply out there just waiting to be vacuumed out of the wallets of Mr. and Mrs. Taxpayer. After all, the federal deficit is just a number to many of those in Congress who are tasked with enacting government finances for the next fiscal year.

If power is an aphrodisiac, I'm truly surprised that those in Washington who play with taxpayer funds as if they were Monopoly money and determine which of their favored constituencies can pay them back with the largest number of re-election votes don't have eight-child families. Many courageous officeholders have made the demand that the federal government stop with the pork projects already, including some of the freshman legislators elected in 2010, but unfortunately they're still a tiny minority who don't have the seniority to take on the Beltway establishment. That's something the public can change pretty easily but they also have to change how they look at the so-called gifts that come to the district courtesy of their Congressman or Senator.

Unfortunately, passing out money from Washington has long been the surest way to get yourself another term in office. Just recall the first exercise in "economic stimulus" that Congress passed in early 2008. What began as a relatively limited scope of targeted tax refunds and reforms (that is, if you consider about $150 billion in this era of budgets which are rapidly approaching $4 trillion as "limited") blossomed into a giveaway incorporating additional unemployment benefits, money for seniors who didn't originally qualify for the tax refunds, assistance on heating bills, and several other layers of lard slathered onto a package that economic conservatives already weren't enamored with.

And when that initial spending didn't work, Congress and both the Bush and Obama Administrations really turned on the spending faucet full-bore and shoveled over $2 trillion into various stimulus programs, a Keynesian dream come true. We've bailed out banks, large insurance companies, two of the Big Three automakers, state governments – the list goes on. But surprisingly to the so-called economic experts running the show, the economy is little improved four years on and unemployment has stayed stubbornly high – something the "stimulus" was supposed to fix. One thing all this spending did fix was the apathy among the American populace as the stimulus packages were one root cause of those gatherings which began both the TEA Party and Occupy movements.

What they may not have figured into these continuing short-term attempts at a fix are the more lasting effects. For one thing, the additional debt created by the stimulus program has to be held by someone. China is one of many foreign nations which hold a staggering amount of our capital in the Treasury bonds we purchase our borrowing power with. Our dealings in trade and with our military might be adversely affected because other nations maintain control over the debts we've accrued. That which we owe can become a weapon used against us just as much as Iran going nuclear or the Chinese rattling their sabers over Taiwan or Tibet, particularly as our nation's debt was downgraded for the first time in our history in 2011. Standard & Poor's lowered our rating because no deal to sufficiently cut spending was reached by Congress that summer.

The second problem we face with artificial stimulus is in reducing risk too much. Most of the time when one ventures their capital into a new idea or project, they understand there is a risk involved. (Read on for some exceptions to the rule.) In a normal economic climate, if I sink my fortune into a company who promises a cure for cancer I'm betting the money I provide will be returned many times over once said cure hits the market and works as desired. Those who invested in Microsoft early on saw that sort of result. Conversely, people who invested in one of the many companies and products which proved to be flops licked their wounds and hopefully resolved to be more careful and studious the next time.

Of course, there are instances where risk is practically removed thanks to government tinkering with the market, with the most egregious example being something I mentioned a chapter ago, Solyndra. This California-based solar panel manufacturer was supported to the tune of $532 million in taxpayer-backed loans just a few short months before its management pulled the plug in August 2011. The shutdown left over 1,000 employees high and dry, while the company's executives refused to answer questions before a Congressional hearing by citing their Fifth Amendment protection against self-implication. Moreover, it was later learned that certain connected private investors would be made whole before taxpayers would retrieve a dime of the failed company's assets.

Unfortunately, this particularly deep and broad-based economic recession which all these stimulus packages and jobs bills have attempted to address has a lot to do with government trying to cover a bad bet by thousands of mortgage lenders and housing speculators that the real estate market would continue on a dizzying upward spiral. When the housing bubble burst, many who bet on the equity in their homes providing the cushion for a lifestyle better than their incomes could handle faced the prospect of foreclosure – joining a huge number of people who were more prudent but who still lost jobs in the continuing economic downturn.

In turn, because those properties didn't hold the inflated value that was placed on them by speculative creditors, mortgagors were left holding the bag. Without mortgage payments coming in, and holding houses and land that wouldn't sell for enough to cover what was owed, lenders were forced to write down billions in debt. Enter the federal government and their taxpayer-funded "stimulus."

The sad fact is much of the original stimulus money – remember that $600 or $1200 check individual taxpayers who qualified received back in 2008, to the tune of about $150 billion from the federal treasury? – simply went back to creditors because people took the "free" money from the government and used it to pay their overdue bills. There was no lesson learned by the recipients about living within their means, nor did the lenders take to heart the fact that perhaps they need to be more careful about loaning their capital without proof of income or good collateral. (Unfortunately, government also played a role in making those lenders assume risks they wouldn't ordinarily take in the name of "promoting home ownership.") Later attempts to stimulate and jumpstart a moribund economy simply bypassed the public for the most part and went directly to the financial institutions in question.

Even with all that, inevitably there will be a "next time" unless attitudes change, both within government and among the general public. We don't tend to maintain our knowledge of hard economic lessons for long, and while we once laughed at the frugality of those who grew up in the Depression we don't anymore because many of us have seen our own hard times. For many of us this small taste of what our grandparents or great-grandparents went through eighty years ago has been quite bitter.

Overall, the 2008 stimulus plan under President Bush and the targeted tax cuts President Obama campaigned on are still more illustrations of the decades-long trend of the federal government tinkering with the budget and tax system to make them work in such a way that fewer and fewer people share the cost of running the government while federal largess is spread out among a larger and larger group of voters. If you've attended a TEA Party or bought this book, chances are you're one who's shouted, "Enough!"

I talked about limiting the role of government in my last chapter. In looking at the bigger picture, the twin ideas of limiting the role that government can take in our lives and having government be fiscally responsible might seem akin to the old chicken-and-egg argument, as in which comes first? In fact, one could theoretically occur without the other but it would be difficult for a leaner entity of government to hold as much force over the individual because of its diminished resources and amount of pork-barrel spending to be given out, nor would a government that respects its limitations be nearly as prone to regularly overspending.

Because enumerated powers are given to the federal government in the Constitution with the balance allocated to the states and people, my focus in this chapter went to the federal level of government. Certainly states share some guilt in this too, but by and large they've prostrated themselves at the altar of the almighty federal government handout and are among the entities waiting in line for their own bailouts because all that the federal government has already given then still wasn't enough to satisfy their free-spending ways. Yet financial reform at the federal level first is what's needed if the taxpayers are ever to get the true relief I outline here.

I'll get back to taxation later in this book, but the next few chapters are going to take a critical look at some of the excesses Washington has enacted and what principles must be followed to reduce their impact to that which is appropriate. In many cases, the proper amount of impact is none whatsoever.

9

Social Security

A facet of the plan I outline in this book that's going to take a combination of diligence, guts, and sacrifice shared by future generations is embodied in what I'd like to see done with the Social Security program. I feel the time has come for the Social Security entitlement to be sunsetted.

There. I've said it.

Indeed, since I'm not a politician I can afford to touch that third rail. And all of you in the AARP can bitch and complain about this chapter to your heart's content, but I'm not going to listen. In fact, I'm going to give the AARP a succinct piece of advice – when I become eligible to join your organization in a few short years (it is age 50, right?) just save yourself the mailing because I'm going to tell you to drop dead.

Of course I know that there's millions of people out there, many of whom are reading this book, who draw a Social Security check. It's a group which includes my parents, who may wonder where they went wrong with their middle son. Certainly I'm aware they were promised benefits for placing their taxes in the trust of the government for all those years they worked. The first thing I'll do in this chapter is some simple math to bust the myth is that you're only receiving the money you put into Social Security. To debunk that fallacy, I ran some basic numbers at the Social Security website.

Using my personal information and my actual age (I'll turn 48 this year) I calculated my benefits due based on three figures: that of a laborer who made just $30,000 in their last year, a middle manager making $60,000 per year, and a six-figure "executive" salary.

As for my $30,000 laborer, they'd only receive $1,064 per month if they retired at age 62. But sticking it out through age 67 would make the financial picture a bit rosier at $1,513 per month, while the "reward" for working through age 70 would be $1,876 per month. Adjusting the income numbers to those of mid-level management types making $60,000 a year would revise the monthly check they could expect upward to $1,306 for retirement at age 62, $1,941 per month four years later, and a whopping $2,431 per month for leaving the workforce at age 70.

Even those who draw a six-figure salary will have a significant loss of earning power by relying on Social Security alone after age 70, as their high end is just $2,838 a month. In terms of a base salary, that's almost like going back to the income level of the aforementioned laborer.

After I found out these stellar income numbers, my next step was to find the tax rates for each year an imaginary worker was employed in a job which paid him the 2012 equivalent of $60,000 per year, using 1970 as a starting point, and adjusting the figures each year as the FICA tax rates increased up to the current 6.2% rate in effect since 1990. (Note that I do not factor in the additional Medicare tax; however, I deducted 2% for 2011 and 2012 because of current Social Security tax breaks in effect.)

Assuming this worker had retired at the age of 62, it would have taken the first 12 years of his or her career to reach the point where his yearly taxes would roughly equal one month's current benefit of $1,306. Further, that first month's benefit nearly exceeds all of the money this laborer had taken out in FICA taxes during his first three working years. All told in this particular case, the total income works out to $1,502,293 while the Social Security tax paid by this mythical worker comes out to $87,364. (The cost of living calculations to work backwards from 2012 came from the American Institute for Economic Research, which has a handy calculator on its website, www.aier.org.)

So if you assumed the monthly benefit of $1,306 were to stay constant – not the best of assumptions since more often than not there's an annual COLA increase to Social Security recipients – it would take this retiree just 67 months to pull out everything they had put into Social Security during a period of over four decades when they earned over $1.5 million. After that, people are basically living on house money, so to speak.

Regardless of the exact numbers, it's nearly as certain as death and taxes that living past retirement age and drawing monthly Social Security benefits for more than 5 years or so fully exhausts every dime of the resources placed into it by a worker. Even if you figure in a modest amount of interest on the money invested, such as that you'd find on an old-fashioned passbook savings account, there are still many millions of seasoned citizens out there who have pulled out every dime they put into the system and are now living in the good graces of those working. So much for that mythical account with your name on it.

To make this personal, I found my own Social Security report, the one the federal government is supposed to send all of us on an annual basis. By looking at that I found that well over $45,000 has been extracted from my paychecks during the years I've been gainfully employed. I don't know about you, but I would've liked to have that extra 45 grand or so during the time because I'm not too confident I'll see it when I'm supposed to – well, unless they follow my idea, in which case there's a fighting chance.

In his first term President George W. Bush introduced a measure which sort of took my idea halfway, embracing the concept of personal Social Security accounts where those who put the money in actually have a say in how it's invested. Of course, because of the radical principle that since this money really belongs to those who earned it they should have a say in where it goes, the Democrats and the AARP (but I repeat myself) accused President Bush of attempting to destroy Social Security.

Well, both of those entities can go ahead and accuse me of that same crime because in this case you would be correct! I definitely want to put an end to the program. Since I see nothing regarding Social Security in my copy of the Constitution, I assert that the federal government had no business in the first place getting into retirement accounts, and further state that much of the entitlement mentality plaguing America today can be traced back to the creation of the Social Security program as part of FDR's New Deal.

On the other hand, there are many millions of Americans who bought into the myth of a Social Security trust fund and believed that this program would assure them their promised benefits upon retirement, so they went on their merry spendthrift way and didn't put anything away for their future. Because of this sad fact, I also know the program can't just be killed in one fell swoop. Instead Social Security has to "wither on the vine," just as onetime Speaker of the House Newt Gingrich was (falsely) accused of saying about Medicare.

A second, and much larger, issue with sunsetting the Social Security program is that the federal government takes the money that is ostensibly withdrawn from your paycheck to supplement your income in later years and spends that cash on things not associated with Social Security. More people have become aware of this in recent years but may not realize that tapping into Social Security for general government spending became standard operating practice beginning in the late 1960's. A vast portion of the impending problem with the program has to do with this incessant raiding of this (so-called) "Social Security Trust Fund." To the feds, it's free money with the added benefit of being off-budget.

I'm writing this book under the assumption that the reader would like to stick around to see the end result of this plan being followed, as I certainly do. However, this creates another side of the oncoming Social Security crisis: simply put, people are living longer, which means, as I demonstrated above, they collect funds well over the sum collected from FICA taxes deducted out of their paychecks for 35 or 40 years. Someone who is lucky enough to reach the century mark could spend over 1/3 of their lifespan collecting Social Security checks without putting anything new into the system. More and more, we see people now being retired from their jobs and collecting benefits for a longer time than they were in the workforce. This is particularly true with women who took a few years away from work to raise their children.

We're rapidly approaching a point where the benefits of one retiree come out of the paycheck of just two workers. This practice all but killed the pension funds of the Big Three automakers, and despite the fact that the federal government has its own monetary printing press this Social Security Ponzi scheme (correctly identified as such by Texas Governor Rick Perry during his 2012 Presidential bid) may spell the end of our prosperity as well.

So something needs to be done. Obviously I have the strongest medicine, which comes as a poison pill to the program. While my approach is somewhat arbitrary, at least I'm placing an idea in the hopper which I think merits study.

The first thing which I propose is fairness to those I described above as trusting in the federal government to supplement their golden years with a monthly stipend. Anyone who collects Social Security now or would become eligible to in the fairly short-term future may retain their full promised benefits, along with the standard cost-of-living adjustments made each year. (That allowance, better known as COLA, has drawn its own fire because there was no increase in 2010 or 2011 because government calculations showed the Consumer Price Index did not increase. A 2010 proposal to buy senior votes was a one-time $250 stipend for those on Social Security to make up for the lack of a COLA.)

People of a certain age who were suckered into the thought that they would have their retirement supplemented by Social Security shouldn't have that rug pulled out from under them, and I fully understand this. However, for those not yet of an age to be eligible for benefits (as of this writing, benefits begin at age 62 for those not collecting Social Security as a disability payment) I would propose that upon their first application they can choose an opt-out option where they receive back the full amount they placed into the system as a nontaxable lump sum; in exchange they'd forego that monthly check the rest of their life. This would be useful to some who are shrewd investors or may be in failing health to a point where they're not likely to make it too long past retirement. As a point for argument I'd say those born prior to 1955 would be entered into this group.

For those born between 1955 and 1965, there are still several prime earning years remaining and they'll have time enough to sock money away in a retirement account. (As part of this the IRS has liberalized IRA rules for that age group and made larger contributions tax-free.) So benefits for this group would be lessened on a sliding scale depending on date of birth, I'd say 75% to 85% of full benefits. Those in Generation X would have their promised benefits decline at an accelerating rate, so eventually those born around 1985 or so would be left with zero. I would also decrease the age where those who chose to could opt out of the system, to the point where the program does wither on the vine because fewer and fewer are eligible to collect benefits and many of those who were given the option chose at an earlier age to opt out in favor of keeping their money and prudently investing it. Eventually as fewer and fewer retirees receive benefits the FICA tax rates for those remaining in the labor force would go down.

(I am making a huge leap of faith on this portion of the plan, as I'm also assuming the federal government can keep its hands off this rich source of revenue. But switching to another taxation basis as I propose in Chapter 13 may help – not to mention getting us back to what the federal government is supposed to be spending our money on!)

However, it's likely no one born today would actually pay zero in FICA taxes for their working life because more people reach a riper old age. As I noted earlier, someone who's 100 years old right now may have been collecting benefits for close to forty years and more people than ever reach the century mark.

While the solution on the survivors' benefits aspect of Social Security is a little less cut and dried, it would also need to have some sort of cutoff; perhaps a similar sliding scale to the retirement supplement portion would be sufficient. Obviously those liberal types who despise the insurance industry would scream because Big Insurance would reap the benefits from this part of my idea, but like I said the government should have never gotten into the insurance business anyway.

The situation we find ourselves in took generations to develop, as the behemoth we know as Social Security started almost eighty years ago, so it'll take at least two generations to restore sanity to the system and bring to a close this long, sad era of dependence on a nanny state to provide income for one's golden years. I'm counting on the next two generations to have the guts and foresight to make a few small sacrifices in order to move the federal government out of a role it never should have adopted.

The next chapter will continue in the same vein about another entitlement program.

10

Health Care

I've said it before and I'll say it again: Health care is NOT a right.

Among the events which turned the TEA Party movement from a few scattered, one-shot protests into a gathering political force was the continuing debate over health care reform in Congress. The summer of 2009 was best known politically for its contentiousness as Democratic members of Congress returned to their home states and districts to hold town hall meetings only to find themselves ambushed by hundreds of protesters who in many cases were better informed about the reform bills than the legislators were. Some elected officials were forthright in their responses but others saw what was happening and attempted to pack these gatherings with large numbers of union members and other special interest supporters of Obamacare. Some representatives refused to have their town hall meetings recorded or allow anything but written questions approved in advance.

This chapter may sound suspiciously like my last chapter on Social Security because the solution is pretty much the same: it's time to get the federal government out of the health care arena too. But instead of a gradual sunsetting of the program as I suggested for Social Security, the Medicare and Medicaid programs would likely be better served by turning them over to each individual state and letting them set their methods of payment, rules, and regulations. (Something about the Ninth Amendment.) Thus the federal government wouldn't be sending states billions to assist with their existing health care and health insurance program costs as a pass through while maintaining their cut.

Moreover, because many states require a balanced budget, returning health care to the states will bring the debate on what should be done about the issue of government involvement in health care and how to pay for it to each state capital. It will beat the current philosophy of just depending on the bottomless well of the federal government to cover the shortfall as states currently do.

But consider how many other issues of import affect our health care system as well.

Illegal immigration has forced a number of hospitals and emergency rooms in the Southwest to close as they were not being compensated for giving care to a horde of people who had no means to pay the providers for their services.

Privacy advocates fret that electronic medical records can be a treasure trove of information for those who want to do us harm, whether through the more sinister aspects of rationing care or the more simple threat of identity theft and pilfering of personal data.

Without tort reform, doctors practice what's known as "defensive medicine," ordering unneeded tests and procedures to build a case in their defense if they're brought to court.

Like the six degrees of Kevin Bacon most issues in the national spotlight can touch on health care sooner or later. Solving the issue will take a coordinated effort across many fields; paying for it is my focus here.

But where does the money come from? While there's been the claim of up to 47 million uninsured Americans bandied about over recent years, the reality is that under federal law no one can be denied care based on inability to pay. It's this factor which leads to the illegal immigrant example above, a factor that is particularly acute in the obstetrics field because thousands of pregnant women cross the border to give birth. These "anchor babies" are considered American citizens by virtue of their being born here.

Leaving non-citizens aside, most Americans have their health care paid for either through employer-sponsored private insurance where the employer may cover all or part of the premium, or through a government program like Medicare, Medicaid, or similar programs run by the individual states. All of these concepts date back decades.

Back when America was fighting World War II, the federal government instituted a number of economic policies to help in focusing production on those items needed to wage a war on two fronts. One of those policies was a wage freeze, and because the automotive unions could not secure additional wages for their members who were still working in Detroit, the sweetener for their wartime labor deal was having the company pay for employees' health insurance. (Bear in mind that at the time these policies were akin to the catastrophic insurance one would get with a health savings account, a point I'll touch on later in this chapter.) Once this became part of the labor deal for a particular group, others began clamoring for it too. Eventually most union deals included employer-paid health insurance and other companies who wished to attract skilled employees eventually followed suit.

The problem rearing its ugly head for the Detroit automakers in recent years was trying to make a profit with the huge amounts being spent on health care for not just their employees, but workers' families and company retirees as well. Instead of running an auto company, Big Three executives complained they were running a health insurer that happened to build cars.

To address that, a recent labor deal allowed the United Auto Workers union to take over this function; in return, the Big Three set up a multi-billion dollar fund as seed money for the program. This enabled Detroit to shave at least some of the price disadvantage they face against foreign automakers, the portion simply based on health insurance costs. But it's a cost of doing business where increasing health insurance premiums have forced many an employer to choose between keeping a certain level of benefits or a certain number of workers.

Switching gears and turning back the clock to the simpler time of the Sixties, the effort by President Lyndon Johnson known as the

Great Society ushered in the current era of health care paid for by our tax dollars. While some on the Republican side vehemently disagreed with the enactment of Medicare and Medicaid as an adjunct to the Social Security program, it was very difficult to argue against a set of programs which were meant for the poor and elderly populations without appearing to be mean-spirited. It was a case, proponents argued, of the government stepping in where the market had not because health insurance for the elderly was difficult to come by in the private market of the time.

Not surprisingly, as generally happens with government estimates, their vision of the price tag was woefully low from day one. People who used to have to scrape up what little money they had just to see a doctor now could go for what they considered free, and they took full advantage of the system.

In both cases, more tinkering around the edges by governmental entities at all levels like mandating certain types of insurance coverage, revising eligibility requirements, changing payments to providers, the advent of health maintenance organizations, and the like have created the monster occupying the nightmares of many Americans who get sicker from dealing with the health care industry than they ever were with their physical ailment.

For over a decade, the standard Beltway liberal proposals had been to essentially expand the original Great Society programs of Medicare and Medicaid to every American regardless of age or income. They have succeeded for the most part by placing children and certain young adults in a similar program called SCHIP, which was adopted in 1997, and expanding the age children could be covered under a parent's health policy to 26 as part of Obamacare. They point to countries like Canada and Great Britain that have been "progressive" enough to adopt a socialized single-payer health care program. However, examples are legion of Canadians who didn't wish to wait weeks or months to have procedures done, instead coming to the United States to get the care that they needed. (One newsworthy case was that of former Newfoundland Premier Danny Williams, who came to the United States in 2010 to have heart surgery performed.) The single-payer system makes for a fatally flawed market that shortchanges both patients and caregivers and is no solution for our nation.

In the meantime, some states have made attempts to change the system from another side by focusing on the health insurance aspect. Probably the most well-known is the Massachusetts plan that GOP Presidential nominee Mitt Romney shepherded through in 2006. In simple terms, Bay State residents either need to have health coverage through their employer, through the state (for unemployed or poorer residents), or pay a penalty with their income taxes.

Many compare the Massachusetts plan to a state's requirement motorists carry auto insurance, but there's one piece of the puzzle that tends to be forgotten. People can get along in life without owning a car (hey, the Amish do it) and, particularly for those who are young and relatively healthy, many don't feel the need for health insurance. The Massachusetts plan compels people who might not want a product to buy it anyway as the price for living in the state. While it's their right as one of the several states, I tend not to agree with governmental mandates of this sort.

Nor does the market, as the Massachusetts plan has been plagued by cost overruns and hasn't insured all state residents, albeit a small percentage of the uninsured are those who would rather forgo the insurance and pay the tax penalty.

Although the Obamacare program wasn't sold that way – and was argued throughout to not be a tax – the recent Supreme Court decision paving the way for full adoption of Obamacare was essentially decided on the same basis that Massachusetts uses to legitimize its program. The Roberts majority decision deemed that not having health insurance could be penalized through the tax code, giving Congress an opening to change or eliminate Obamacare entirely, but also enshrining the further use of the IRS as a provider of punishment if left unchecked.

Yet another factor in any discussion of health care is the effect of prescription drugs on medical treatment. Obviously, people want to live longer and enjoy a better quality of life. Compared to our ancestors, we live much longer and in general have healthier lives because many of the diseases and ailments which plagued earlier generations have been eradicated or controlled. Going under the knife used to be a risky proposition because of the possibility of infection, but now millions do it simply for vanity reasons or to improve their eyesight because of advances in both the procedures themselves and in the disease-fighting medications available to the patient. In fact, the need for many surgeries has been eliminated by the creation of medicines to combat chronic diseases.

And the role of pharmaceuticals has evolved from being a lifesaver like penicillin was when it was introduced in the mid-20th century to the common usage of those medications devoted simply to improving one's perceived quality of life, such as Rogaine or Viagra – both examples of research by pharmaceutical manufacturers who found these medicines didn't work as well as others for their originally intended purposes, but there were beneficial side effects associated with them.

With these advances in modern medicine it followed that this vital portion of modern health care became squeezed in much the same way that health insurance and paying for basic care were. To stay competitive, employers added coverage for prescription drugs to their health insurance plans. With the federal government already involved in Medicare, President George W. Bush and Congress pushed through the Medicare Part D program which entwined Uncle Sam even deeper into the internal business of Big Pharma. That program is another Gordian knot we'll have to figure out how to untie in dealing with the entirety of the health care issue.

And it goes without saying that the sad thing about Medicare Part D is many of its recipients didn't need this program expansion because they dealt with the issue through private means. Unfortunately, they will have to live with and pay for it anyway. Instead of leaving well enough alone, or, even better, allowing the states to propose their own solutions, American taxpayers became stuck with yet another federal entitlement program.

So you've read several pages outlining the myriad problems with our nation's health care system. But to me, the system itself isn't broken and we don't have to throw the baby out with the bathwater to address the issue. What it will take is shifting the cost and responsibility for life choices to the end user, while in return the federal government lightens the burden on all of us by exiting the health care field insofar as it possibly can, excepting its obligations to our veterans. A good place to start is dropping the Part D prescription program and allowing the private sector to get back into that market, allowing competition and choice once again without the federal regulation overkill.

With the income tax system we presently have, I think the best interim solution to cutting the cost of physician and hospital care is to allow health savings accounts (HSA) to become easier to get and more accessible. This would require some quick action, though, as the   HSA is an endangered species under Obamacare.

In general, the HSA is treated like an IRA for tax purposes and is combined with a high-deductible medical insurance plan. While it seems like a pretty good idea on the surface, the problem is that not all health insurance providers cater to the HSA market. Also, many states still mandate certain coverage types which may or may not apply to the individual case. Perhaps by removing the insurance component from the savings account we could get better participation by the population at large, particularly those who are just starting out in the workforce and may not work for an employer who provides that benefit. While the insurance aspect could be encouraged through some sort of financial incentive, if folks wanted to go without and participate they still could.

It's a step toward the overall solution that I addressed at the top because the shift from federal to state responsibility cannot happen overnight. Nor can the federal government truly divest itself from being a health care provider unless it decides to turn over the care of our veterans in a similar matter, and that incentive of federally-provided health care is one strong motivation for men and women of the generation growing up now to sign up and serve in the military. With the Long War and terrorism a threat for the foreseeable future, it may be beyond the reach of the next generation or two to totally devolve Washington from health care.

However, I do think that there's a part of addressing the issue of health care that won't take years to enact; in fact, it should take about the length of time it takes to read and comprehend the next few sentences. Just like the fiscal responsibility discussion that I wrote about early on in this book, there's an element of personal accountability that becomes part of this solution too.

For example, one aspect of attempting to drive down health care costs is a business choosing not to allow smoking on its premises. While I don't think the nanny state should have a say in this (even though many states already do) it's just fine for a private entity to do so. And being a guy who likes tasty food, I'm not in favor of banning transfats but common sense dictates that if you slam down two Whoppers and a king-size order of fries on a regular basis, you'll get to be obese and that's not a particularly healthy thing because being overweight can be a trigger for a number of life-threatening diseases.

The best way to avoid the steep cost of health care, particularly the high-dollar results of cardiac treatment or combating diabetes, is to live in a reasonably healthy manner. It's a shame to me that kids today are already too portly for their own good because of a sedentary lifestyle. As a kid, I was out the door like a shot during the summer, out riding my bike or playing sandlot baseball. While the dregs of society have dictated a few changes to the world kids live in today, it's not impossible for a kid to get outside and as my dad would say, "have the stink blown off" him or her. Nor would it hurt the parents to do the same.

It's those kids of today sitting in front of their video games or surfing the Internet who are going to have to deal with the health care woes of people my age. I wouldn't like to see their paychecks eroded as badly as mine is now to deal with the federal government's "one-size-fits-all" solution but if we don't act quickly those in power inside the Beltway will see to it that we're saddled in just such a manner through Obamacare and its associated taxes and red tape.

While getting these kids off their posteriors and actually doing some physical activity is one thing, seeing to their education is quite another. That's what I'll look at in the next chapter.

11

Education

From the earliest days of our nation, the federal government has taken an interest in education. The Northwest Ordinance (1787) expressed the philosophy in one phrase:

Religion, morality, and knowledge, being necessary to good government and the happiness of mankind, schools and the means of education shall forever be encouraged.

If things had stopped there, I don't think there would have been a need for me to write this chapter. In today's schools, though, one is led to wonder if the goal is to educate children or to maintain a requisite number of reasonably cushy administrative positions.

Test scores in general have either declined or held steady over the last few decades, while the testing isn't considered as rigorous as it once was. The forces of political correctness have determined that standardized testing is unfair to poor and minority students and demand changes regularly. And some parents consider the school a babysitting and restaurant service, since most serve free or reduced-price meals, not caring much about how their children progress or behave at school.

Some of these complaints were addressed under President George W. Bush as the No Child Left Behind Act was shepherded through Congress early in his first term and signed in January 2002. While Bush asked for this act to combat what he termed "the soft bigotry of low expectations", it also added more federal regulations to the multitude that already exist, and became a target for Democrats to constantly claim that NCLB was underfunded.

While I appreciate a set of measurable standards for school performance, in reality this law hasn't done a whole lot to improve the learning status of America's children and took even more away from the concept of local control. In my opinion, the law to its full extent wasn't necessary and it encourages education in exactly the opposite manner from what it should be.

I was educated in public schools for the 13 years of my primary and secondary schooling, and graduated from a public state university. There was a period in elementary school where I was in a special class because I have what's now known as ADHD, and I finished my high school years by taking vocational classes for my junior and senior years related to the art and technique of architectural drafting. Throw in a move my parents made during my formative years which took me from a city school district to a rural one and I experienced a number of different classroom situations, perhaps moreso than the average child.

What the schools taught me was all of the factual knowledge I needed to get through and get a good grade point average. History and math classes were pretty much a piece of cake for me and I did reasonably well in English. (Imagine that.) Science was pretty easy as well.

One disadvantage I had, though, was spending my middle and high school years in a small, rural district where few advanced classes were offered. (Though, to be fair, I went to vocational school so I didn't opt to stay and take some of the AP classes that may have been available to me in 11th and 12th grade.) Conversely, my daughter, the young lady to whom I dedicated this work, received a chance to participate in a gifted/talented program because she went to school in a large city district and took advantage of several of these classes to get her high school language credits during her junior high years.

But there were two things I learned in college that I never did in high school. One was how to study and manage time because I didn't have to do that for most of my previous academic career. The other was something I'm still learning to some extent – as most of us eventually do – and that's the art of critical thinking.

Teaching to the test in the manner to which most schools are geared simply allows a child to regurgitate the facts they're taught without giving those lessons a context to work from. This particularly affects kids when they're taught history and current events.

For example, if children are taught American history, they brush through the saga of the Pilgrims coming to America. If anything, they're taught about all of the help the Indians gave the settlers and how they thanked the Indians by holding a Thanksgiving feast. They learn nothing about the reason the Pilgrims came (religious persecution in Europe) or of the failure of the colonists' early efforts at communal living. Their bountiful harvests came after they abandoned their socialistic practices and allowed each settler to keep and trade their own land and labor. Unfortunately, this and many other important parts of early American history are barely covered in schools today.

There's also the question of ever-spiraling educational budgets that seem to take more and more of a bite of our wallets. Well over 2/3 of the money a school district spends is in the form of salaries and benefits. True, a good teacher is worth every penny he or she is paid, but too many teachers simply go there to collect a paycheck – and in extreme cases, due to union contracts, are paid despite not teaching at all! While they've been proven to be a danger to children, union rules in some districts make it all but impossible for the school district to let them go.

The first part of my educational plan looks at the monetary issues school systems grapple with.

I strongly believe that since it's we the taxpayers who provide the money to educate the majority of our children, any money spent on education at the state or local level should follow the child. Whether it's through vouchers or some other sort of market-based mechanism, giving this power of the purse to parents will encourage schools to become better or lag behind the market.

Nor do I mind the idea of for-profit schools. I understand that some will argue that educating a child is nothing like running a business to make money. It's a logical argument to some extent but the contention has one major flaw.

Before children are sent to the school system, they remain in the care of the parents or legal guardians unless they choose to delegate that task to someone else. Obviously one choice that is made – for the most part by mothers, but the occasional father does this, too – is to remain at home and take care of the child. Of course, other families or single parents who feel they can't afford this option usually place the child in day care of some sort. Many times it's a willing relative but on most occasions parents look for what they consider the best day care center their budget allows. In that case, the provider is looking to make their living or secure a profit for the entity they're employed by. In other words, day care is a business too, so why not allow this type of competition for educating a child? It would also create new opportunities for teachers who excel at their craft, a point I'll revisit shortly.

Another piece of this financial puzzle comes as a message to those inside the Beltway: there's no amendment in our Constitution which mandates the federal government either pays for education or hangs the sword of Damocles over local school districts by forcing them to do what the feds want – including No Child Left Behind. So butt out of the education business!

There's already way too much bureaucracy at the local and state levels for the system's own good, and having a federal layer tossed on top just creates a lot of make-work positions for pencil-pushers who are about as far removed from educating a child as we are from the moon. In short, our so-called Department of Education should cease to exist. Unfortunately, dismantling that department and its bureaucracy was something President Reagan promised but failed to deliver, yet the argument for eliminating the DOE remains just as valid thirty years later.

Secondly, the next two generations need to address the curriculum taught to their children, whether in the public schools or within other educational avenues. It goes without saying that there should be more local input; however, as a parent who had children in school not too many years ago I've seen some of the strange items they were taught. Unfortunately most parents are too trusting of their school systems and don't take a closer look at the lesson plans intended for their children's malleable minds. It's my hope that introducing market forces to a larger extent will assist parents in making better school choices, which can and should include locally-controlled public schools.

Because while Johnny is learning about how to put condoms on a cucumber, absorbing convenient myths about anthropogenic global warming, or pretending to be Islamic for a week, there are a number of more valuable subjects the schools don't take the time to cover. Just ask today's average high school student a question in the areas of American history, geography, or economics. While many do get some amount of instruction in those areas, it's surely not uncommon to get an incorrect answer or simply a blank stare. Moreover, given the writing and speaking skills I see and hear out of a lot of today's youth, proper English needs to be revived as well.

As I foreshadowed a few paragraphs ago, it's my contention that if we can get money to follow the child we would also solve another issue which bedevils the educational world. Teachers who are really good at their craft would have more demand placed for their services; theoretically it could be possible for them to create their own cottage industry blending the best aspects of homeschooling and school-based education by becoming independent contractors. In fact, using this concept I could easily see a private or charter school attracting the best teachers in a particular area, or even teachers becoming entrepreneurs by leasing their own space in a larger school building where the teacher could educate in a way they see fit while reaping full rewards for their excellence.

Imagine a news story along the lines of a star athlete signing a new deal, but instead it's your state teacher of the year making headlines by signing a long-term big-money contract with some charter school. Even a public school could do something like this, but it would likely take a complete streamlining of administration and decertification of the union that bends over backwards to have teachers treated equally regardless of ability or results. I realize this free market idea which doesn't rely on a large union is a stunning concept, which is why the National Education Association and other teachers unions fight against these proposals tooth and nail.

Since I have the opportunity and have grabbed your attention, I also want to extol the virtues of vocational education. As I mentioned, I attended vocational school for my last two years of high school; in my case it taught me a lot about drafting in general and a bit about architecture – very convenient since that was the field I eventually went into and practiced for over twenty years. I think computer-aided drafting was hardly a concept back then; in that era we were still in the Stone Age and I actually learned drafting on a tilted table with a pencil, straightedge, and scads of templates for everything from drawing varied size circles to appliances to lettering. As a group, we were barely removed from the white shirt and tie generation practicing architecture in a room full of drafting boards.

Returning from my quick trip down Memory Lane, my point is that not all kids are the proverbial college material. At the same time, our nation also suffers from an unfortunate shortage of skilled tradesmen. Even though I actually went from a vocational education to a four-year university, most kids may not have that desire and I see nothing wrong with learning to be a CAD operator, plumber, carpenter, or machinist. Given how I did in my junior high shop class I was certainly on the right end of the building industry as far as my skills were concerned, but we simply have too few people who are interested in these sorts of occupations, which can be lucrative in many cases and certainly qualify under the moniker of "honest living." On the other hand we have way too many young people who drift through college not knowing what they want to be, or worse, get through school with aspirations to be a bureaucrat! Better to be a dirt-pusher running a bulldozer than a pencil-pusher whose only running is to the lunchroom for their midday break.

Unfortunately, this advice has come too late for the group of young people who famously declared they were among the "99 percent" and participated in some way with the Occupy Wall Street protests because of their lack of success in getting employment right out of school. But it goes without saying that getting a master's degree in Women's Studies or some other avant-garde major without much of a practical purpose in the real world limits one's job prospects. And I'll just say that many of the Occupiers at Wall Street and other locations may not match the average HR manager's idea of a company's public face. On the other hand, appearance doesn't matter quite so much on a job site as an electrician or heavy equipment operator or repairman.

In short, we need more people who make things or make things work, and that's generally the purpose of vocational education.

I'm sure that 99% of you reading this book agree education should be about what's best for the children. (If not, you probably work for either the Department of Education or a teachers' union.) To that end I believe that the more available options children have in their education, the better they'll eventually succeed in life.

Instead of filling these "skulls full of mush" with just enough facts to pass a standardized test and not impart the context with which these facts fit, we need to teach kids how to think for themselves. As it stands in America today, those environments for learning which tend to show the most success (namely, private schools and homeschooling) generally have the least to do with governmental regulation and the most to do with educating children through more rigid discipline, a course of study emphasizing classical subjects, and a greater sense of morality through faith-based studies.

As a whole I think it will be easier to get to a better educational model that will ably serve for generations to come if those who dictate the rules for how children are taught the skills to serve them best in life are based as closely as possible to those they educate, and not in some Washington D.C. office.

Meanwhile, the end result of education should be to have the best and brightest entrepreneurs and workforce we can. In my next chapter I'll explore how government can help with creating jobs.

12

Trade and Job Creation

To begin this chapter of my book, let me say that I'm in favor of free but fair trade. Maybe not every participant in the TEA Party or Occupy Wall Street will agree with me, but I believe the idea behind NAFTA and other trading alliances is a sound one – although there is definitely some tweaking which needs to be done around the edges. These will be items I'll cover in this chapter.

I don't generally agree with those who are strict protectionists because they don't seem to understand that our economy is a global one and discouraging competition by enacting high tariffs and other barriers to free trade hurts our own economy the most in the long run. This also discourages innovation, which is the key to creating new jobs. I think back to the East German-made Trabant automobile as the poster child for this phenomenon. That car was an ill-fated relic of Communist society which lagged thirty years behind the rest of the automotive world and was abandoned by the free market once Germany reunified.

On the other hand, I also feel that we're giving away too much of our industrial base by shipping the production of these goods out of America. If you purchase an electronic product, chances are it was manufactured in China, and countless other items are made just across our southern border in Mexico. I realize that with the cost of labor becoming more and more a share of the total product price, businesses still need to create profitability for themselves and their stockholders. And I'm definitely a supporter of the American capitalist system because it's been proven to advance our standard of living farther than any other nation could have ever dreamed of in the short timespan America has existed.

All is not negative in the realm of industry, as we do have some bright spots in our manufacturing economy. With our skilled labor force and a prosperous population because of these skills, America still attracts many of the top global industrial giants to our shores; particularly in the automotive field. While the nameplate on the car may have a foreign name like Honda, Kia, Toyota, or BMW, many of their models are assembled right here in America. In turn, these factories spawn thousands more ancillary jobs from both manufacturing of parts and associated service jobs created by the influx of overseas capital.

At this juncture I want to take a look at just a few of the major products that America imports and exports and make my statement on the direction I think we need to go in order to maintain our prosperity despite competition from huge Asian markets like China and India. While I can't cover everything we produce or import because this would become a 500-page chapter, an intelligent reader should be able to deduce from my few examples where our nation needs to go.

The trading commodity arguably most affecting middle America is agriculture. While the romanticized *American Gothic* version of the farmer is long gone and has been replaced by the modern-day Internet-literate farmer with a university degree working on his (or her) multi-thousand acre spread, it's still a fact that American farmers are able to supply our country's basic nutritional needs many times over; in addition they also grow products that in some cases fuel our automobiles. Even with the demand from the energy side, American farmers are still able to send millions of tons of grain around the globe.

Conversely, while America has many areas suitable for citrus crops and truck farming, more and more of those products arrive from overseas. Long gone are the days of "in season" vegetables and fruits. Items are now available year-round both because of rapid air shipment from the Southern Hemisphere and technological advances that enable fruit such as apples to be maintained and retain flavor for much longer periods. Even so, there are some dark clouds on the horizon for which American farmers need to be prepared.

First and foremost, as environmental regulations become more onerous the competitive advantage we enjoy is eroded. Fertilizers may have to change composition, becoming less effective. More regressive restrictions on waste disposal could hamper poultry, pork, and cattle farmers as well as egg producers.

Secondly, while I'm certainly no anti-growth zealot I'm aware that suburban sprawl sometimes takes prime agricultural land out of production. In some cases, though, farmers are prevented from that sometimes necessary option by state regulations, a subject I alluded to back in Chapter 3.

A third pitfall would be the reduction in food yield from the energy side as millions upon millions of bushels of corn exit the food chain and become automotive fuel. Ethanol production continues to increase markedly and, if present trends continue, corn on the cob could become as rare a commodity on the table as fresh strawberries in December used to be. It's also possible that while corn production does increase enough to serve both masters, the additional corn comes at the expense of other important food base products like soybeans or wheat.

As farming continues to evolve into being a less and less labor-intensive task due to the twin influences of technology and a shrinking real number of farms, I believe job creation in the agricultural field needs to be concentrated on research in two realms of study. One path would be to discover ways to make crops more disease-resistant, improve yields, and make them more adaptable to poorer soil conditions. That last point is particularly important as the allowable quantities of both natural and artificial fertilizer decrease because of the pollution in our streams claimed to occur with the overuse of these products.

The second path is searching for ways to make biomass or other agricultural by-products more useful in the energy field as a substitute for the corn most of us like to eat. It's a known fact that methane gas from animal waste is a huge emission source; the trick lies in finding a method to utilize this resource while keeping it out of the watershed.

Turning to the other side of the coin, one vital import of ours is oil. Like ethanol, the role of oil to our energy needs is another subject I'll go into further in Chapter 14. Make no mistake, though, oil is also a relevant subject in this chapter.

On the import side of our trading ledger crude oil dominates the field. Even as America still has a lot of oil left underneath her lands and territorial waters, overblown environmental concerns have prevented us from taking advantage of our own resources. Instead, we now import almost 2/3 of our daily oil consumption. And the list of countries we buy our oil from is a list of those not necessarily in agreement with the strategic goals we've set globally. Since Canada is fuming at us because of the political yo-yo that is the Keystone XL pipeline, we're now at odds in some way, shape or form with our main suppliers of foreign oil.

Further, while oil is generally refined into the fuel that drives our transportation industry, we can't forget that this resource has many other uses, particularly in the manufacture of plastic products. So it's vitally important that we work out some sort of compromise between the environmental issues and the national interest that we all have in maintaining a free supply of domestic oil. Our current situation, where some stalwarts in Congress place the needs of caribou above the needs of our economy, has passed the ridiculous stage and is quickly closing in on dangerous. Even if full access to ANWR, Pacific, and Gulf drilling were allowed tomorrow, we've lost, and will continue to lose in the short-term future, a tremendous amount of capital which could have been left in the domestic realm. Instead, thanks to short-sightedness inside the Beltway, we daily deliver to OPEC their sheik's ransom for black gold.

Once again, technology plays a role in allowing us to begin moving past an oil-based economy. Just like steam-powered vehicles were replaced by gasoline-powered ones early in the 20th century, somewhere out there is the key to the next generation of transport. Until we get to that point, though, and as something that will create a number of high-paying jobs, many of these restrictions on oil exploration and refining need to be lifted.

America does have one export that maybe not everyone thinks of as a commodity, but it creates a huge amount of capital. As a nation, the United States is a world leader in intellectual property – a term I'll adopt as shorthand for all of the books, movies, television, and musical recordings created by Americans and exported around the world. In many cases, revenues made overseas by films can exceed the domestic take, while native musical artists considered obscure here are hugely popular in various foreign nations.

One of our major trade gripes with China and other nations, particularly in Asia, is their laxity when it comes to stopping the sale of pirated movies. Black market copies of Hollywood films are big sellers there but the studios never receive a cut of the take. And with the evolution of "on-demand" movies, downloads of songs for personal use, and increased availability of internet bandwidth, major film studios and record labels are going to find it increasingly difficult to maintain a revenue stream based on models developed 30 to 50 years ago. In fact, the 2007 writers strike in Hollywood hinged largely on this very issue of being compensated for media broadcast via the Internet as opposed to more traditional venues like theaters or television.

On the flip side media has become more accessible than ever. Personally, I know some of my favorite local bands would've had a lot more difficulty having their music heard prior to the advent of Facebook, ReverbNation, and the internet in general. While we have the phoniness of something like "American Idol" (which actually originated "across the pond" in Great Britain) to our discredit there is still quite the demand for all things American and a largely untapped market out there for us to export intellectual property.

At the beginning of this chapter, I promised suggestions on how to "tweak" trade pacts like NAFTA. But maybe tweak isn't a strong enough description because I think a more thorough pruning is in order. There comes a point where an agreement such as NAFTA is less about trade and more about sovereignty, and that's the point where we have to go back to the beginning and ask ourselves what the goal of the agreement was in the first place. A reduction in tariffs to zero between ourselves, Mexico, and Canada is a pretty good idea for the most part. But items like a trade corridor where trucks coming from Mexico don't see a customs stop until they're in the midst of our heartland – friends, that's an invitation to disaster.

We also need to be prepared to do unto others as they do unto us, even if it does risk a larger trade war. We already have an issue with China regarding intellectual privacy, but they also don't play fairly when it comes to manipulating the value of their currency and other aspects of the trade agreements both parties signed. Perhaps it's time to take them back to the drawing board as well.

But in order to rework trade agreements we first need to place ourselves in the position of dealing from strength and not out of weakness. At this point it's fair to complete the circle and discuss our manufacturing capability again, this time by reviewing a little history.

In the century-and-a-quarter from 1845 to 1970, Americans changed the world. Starting with Samuel F.B. Morse revolutionizing communications with the telegraph, on our shores we created invention after invention which made our global society as we know it, even while America fought and won two world wars. In the span of 66 years, this golden era of invention took us from a short machine-powered flight over Kitty Hawk to Neil Armstrong and his small step for man. And while America is still a powerhouse when it comes to innovation, many of the more recent advances have occurred offshore. It sometimes seems to me like we've settled on mediocrity, simply doing research in order to secure the next government grant instead of being truly innovative.

It's long past time for Americans to make stuff again. But the idea in this go-round is not necessarily to make the cheapest product, it's to make the most cutting-edge product that has the quality and construction to last for decades. In turn, American consumers need to reward these efforts and consider quality as much (if not more) than price. Maybe a better term for this consideration is life-cycle cost.

The coming generations have the potential to allow America to be a leader once again, just like it was not all that long ago. Before we cede our crown to those in China or India, we need to remember that there's a reason that Japanese auto makers put their trust in us to build many of their best-selling cars. Japan became a world leader by taking both the American know-how that rebuilt their industry after we defeated them in World War II and the can-do spirit that still existed in America at that time, and allowing these to evolve by putting an emphasis on manufacturing goods of high quality and innovation. We can repeat the process on our own terms by putting our minds to it and telling those who wish for us to remain mediocre, like those interested in big government at the expense of creative capitalism, to get out of the way.

13

Taxation

It's sort of fitting that this chapter is number 13, since there's a segment of the population which fears that generally unlucky number. My personal phobia is one of a society being crushed under the weight of too many taxes, fees, surcharges, tolls, and all the other ways we pay to allow the government to operate. As you can tell by previous chapters, I agree with a lot of conservatives and libertarians who think the government operates in far too many areas. The quality of many tasks done by government is nowhere near that which the ingenuity of the private sector could provide.

We all know that April 15 is a date on the calendar that brings dread to everyone – well, almost everyone. (It's a great day for a TEA Party!) Those who make their living from the business of preparing the millions of tax returns Americans are forced to fill out every year look at that otherwise lovely spring day like retailers look at Christmas Eve – the tail end of their cash cow. Just like the crocuses in spring, tax preparation outfits pop up soon after the calendar year begins in malls and storefronts across the nation, all promising a larger refund than the next guy. Never mind that the so-called "refund" is simply being paid back the money our federal and state governments confiscated out of your paycheck without the benefit of interest. Just try to pay back a mortgage, credit card, or student or car loan like that.

It wasn't always this way. For most of the first 150 years of our nation's history, Washington got along just fine on a revenue stream derived mainly from tariffs on imported goods. There were times when income taxes were forced on the public, but they didn't last for more than a few years. Not until February 3, 1913, one of the darkest days in our nation's history, did it become Constitutionally permissible to tax citizens solely on income. And as it was sold to a skeptical public back in those days, the tax man was only going to take from the richest portion of society. Common laborers and average business owners need not worry, they said. Yeah, right!

Awhile back I read a book that I recommend for anyone who doesn't like the current taxation system: *The FairTax Book* by Neal Boortz and John Linder. You can say what you will about the concept of a national sales tax, also known as a consumption tax, but the argument in favor of this system is well-spelled out in the book. I can't say that I'm a total convert because there is an element of the FairTax called the prebate which still requires income disclosure and reporting, but I do know the system as it stands right now is corrupted, complicated, and I think broken beyond repair. If our tax code were an automobile it would have been eligible for Cash for Clunkers and bound for the scrap heap.

I agree that the progressive tax system that Boortz and Linder currently revile is exactly the wrong approach because I don't fall for the liberal bilge about soaking the rich because they're not giving enough. People who manage to amass wealth generally do it through hard work and I feel that sweat and effort should be rewarded, not punished.

Because of that I've been an advocate of a fairer, flatter tax system for quite awhile. In 1996 and 2000 I was a big Steve Forbes supporter because of his flat tax idea. Former Congressman Dick Armey was another flat tax proponent.

However, as time went on I began seeing a few problems with both the Forbes and Armey approaches. My biggest quandary with their respective methods was that the two key numbers were vulnerable to the whims of Congress, as both the tax rate and the standard deduction could be tweaked. I also knew from lengthy observation of the national political scene that there would be a day when some brilliant mind would come up with just one extra deduction that simply had to be in there, signaling the start to yet another rush back to the system we have now. (In fact, Armey's plan maintained a few cherished deductions.)

So fast forward a decade or so to another Presidential contender, businessman Herman Cain. He created a sensation in his 2012 Presidential run by proposing a hybrid between a flat tax and consumption tax called the 9-9-9 Plan. Like his good friend Boortz, Cain embraced the idea of a consumption tax but knew there had to be a transition toward it, so the idea of 9-9-9 was born. The numbers represented a 9 percent income tax rate for all citizens, a 9 percent business tax rate – as opposed to our current 35% rate – and a 9 percent national consumption tax. Obviously those inside the Beltway who were used to having the power to control behavior through the tax code weren't going to stand idly by while their method of control was taken away, so they roundly panned it.

Another troubling feature of flat tax ideas, and even to an extent the 9-9-9 Plan, was the lack of any effort to end backup withholding. Originally people wrote yearly or quarterly checks to the IRS, similar to the way those who pay estimated tax do now. Backup withholding became law in the World War II era and was sold as a way to ensure a more constant revenue stream to the government for fighting the war. The withholding idea was supposed to be temporary, but like most revenue enhancements "temporary" became permanent in one big hurry once the dollars rolled in and those in charge realized that the golden goose could still be a-layin'. In this case backup withholding wasn't dropped once hostilities ended.

Like the flip side to the age-old financial wisdom about paying yourself first and placing a regular part of your paycheck in some sort of savings or investment account, people don't tend to think about what they pay in taxes because they never actually see the money they would have received. The important number on their paycheck became the net pay and not the gross pay, yet when people talk about what they earn it's almost always in terms of gross pay. Even worse, some actually ask to be taxed at a higher rate to ensure themselves a larger refund check down the road. They forget it's their money in the first place!

Since it's my personal preference, let's say for the sake of this discussion that the FairTax is the way to go. In order to make it effective, the very first task would need to be repealing the Sixteenth Amendment. Obviously the biggest hurdles to that would be *a)* getting a 2/3 majority of each house of Congress to go along with it and *b)* convincing 38 states to do the same. If we ever get through step A I'd be willing to bet a steak dinner at a fancy restaurant that my adopted home state of Maryland would be one of the holdouts insofar as step B goes, as would most of the other states which Democrats hold with an iron fist. The reason repealing the Sixteenth Amendment has to be done first (or concurrently) with adopting a new sales tax system is that I could just see some Democrat saying, ok, you have the FairTax, but we need to keep the income tax around in case we need a backup source of revenue – first chance they get, bam! Double taxation.

While tax cuts can be sold in Congress, as three major ones were over the last thirty years (Ronald Reagan in 1981 and George W. Bush in 2001 and 2003), what seemingly cannot be sold there is the idea of true tax reform. Most in Congress may publicly tell you that their main concern with changing the tax system to one based on consumption, or even one with a flat rate for all taxpayers, is the worry about a stable source of revenue. Particularly when arguing against a consumption tax, they'll point to times like these when consumer spending is down and fret that there wouldn't be enough inflow to the Treasury to maintain vital government programs and services. Despite the fact that many of these programs and services are nowhere near as vital as Congress thinks they are based on my first 12 chapters and beyond, in truth what the current tax code really has become is a full employment act for both the thousands of lobbyists who infest the area inside the Beltway like cockroaches and the crony capitalists who depend on government money to keep their businesses afloat and to line their pockets.

For example, how many groups would be affected by a radical change in tax law like a national consumption tax or a flat tax with limited deductions?

Let's start with the tax preparation industry itself. Simpler forms, or none at all, would put a vast number of those people out of work. Their lobbyists are paid to buttonhole members of Congress with tales of woe about the unfairness of flat tax rates or the financial disaster sure to await if a consumption tax is enacted. Better to maintain the system and maybe tweak it around the edges – oh, and here's a campaign contribution check from our political action committee.

Then it would be the Realtors' turn. Getting rid of the deduction for mortgage interest would destroy the already-battered housing market, they would cry, and it would put a lot of our members out of work because the demand for home ownership would further collapse without the incentive of tax savings. (The temporary tax credit for home buying enacted in 2009 was extended and expanded for this very reason – yet the housing market continued to crater.) They would say, Mr. Congressman, do you want to be the one who denies the American Dream to all those people who buy homes in part because of the tax advantages?

Of course, then the bankers and lenders would chime in because without the tax-deducted home equity loans the banks which still remain after the financial sector's disaster of 2008 would go out of business, those who deal with mutual funds and stocks would lament the loss of 401.(k) and IRA accounts for retirement, lobbyists hired by those tax-favored industries like alternative energy or electric cars would scream about losing that incentive, and so on and so forth. I could probably write another twenty pages about all the groups who would whine and moan about losing their tax breaks should the current system be erased and a do-over placed into effect.

The point is that many in Congress would fight any sort of major tax reform tooth and nail because then they can't divvy out tax breaks like candy to their favored constituencies. And that fact of modern American political life begs several questions.

To start with, is it the duty of government to provide market-busting incentives to promote some action or penalize ideas that lead to vast wealth using the tax code? As just one example, how about tax incentives to those who wanted to build "green" buildings? Is this a noble purpose? Possibly. But shouldn't market forces allow this to happen naturally? After all, if a "green" building provides an energy savings that's worth the extra price, one would think developers would voluntarily rush to adopt all of those standards themselves. Obviously the added cost continues to be a disincentive, or at the very least isn't deemed to have a worthwhile payback period yet.

At all levels of government, getting rid of the usage of the tax code as a carrot or stick is probably the biggest hurdle to any sort of reform. To that end, it's going to take getting a majority in Congress which isn't power-hungry but truly citizen servants. We had a decent start on this in 2010, but that's where the voters in 2012 and beyond need to continue playing a part.

Then there's the element of choice. Another hidden benefit of a tax based on consumption is that, unlike the current system, anyone who receives income from practically any source is not forced to pay it. Every week or two those of us who receive a paycheck find that a significant portion of it has been vacuumed out by the federal and state governments; yes, that backup withholding thing.

Nor does this account for a couple "breaks" many employees receive because their Section 125 flex benefit and 401.(k) plan are pre-tax deductions. Federal tax laws dictate they can't use that money they earned unless certain restrictions are met – in the case of the Section 125 flex benefit they have to spend it on medical-related expenses to be reimbursed at a later date. Most can't touch their 401.(k) without penalty until they turn 59½ years old. (Based on our Social Security woes I outlined in Chapter 9, that may not be such a bad thing. Still, the point remains.)

On the other hand, under a consumption tax people would have the option to pay it if they decide to spend money on new goods. With the somewhat frugal lifestyle many lead they could have less of a tax bite per capita than someone who spends money like water. (That frugal description fits me to a T. And I am quite aware that, in this economy of ours that's extraordinarily dependent on consumer spending, I'm not pulling my weight. Deal with it.)

It's the element of choice I have in the matter which makes a consumption tax appeal most to me. Right now I have the hollow "choice" of paying taxes or being financially ruined by the IRS. In my case it would be difficult, to say the least, to do my outside job from the federal pen. I also have a sneaking hunch the feds would frown on me writing a blog from the cell block too, particularly one which is Exhibit A of my attitude toward Big Government.

If you look at all of the preceding 12 chapters of this tome you'll see that there's one underlying theme tying them all together, and that theme will continue on through the remainder of this book.

I want the next generations of Americans to enjoy more of the benefits of freedom and endure less of the oppression of an ever-expanding federal government. In this case, it's the freedom to keep more of what our progeny will earn if they choose to. I'm also aware that they'll have to fight for their freedoms against many and varied enemies, not just from outside our nation, but some silver-tongued devils from within who will be seductive in their promises of equality for all.

As a nation we should strive for equality of opportunity. But we have to guard against the big-government do-gooders who preach equality of outcome and have the means to redistribute wealth in a vain attempt to insure it. Just like in George Orwell's *Animal Farm*, those in power have the tendency to consider themselves more equal than others and exempt themselves and those they favor from the rules the rest of us have to live by. For these crony capitalists, the tax code is a favorite weapon.

If I live to see another 50 years, all I ask is that those generations yet to be born have the freedom and ability to live and succeed as far as their talents, abilities, and knowledge take them. To that end, job one is to assure them that they will be able to enjoy the fruits of their labor by not having an increasingly large portion of it confiscated for redistribution to those who, for whatever reason, haven't succeeded as well. I implore those next two generations to show me the American Dream envisioned by the Founding Fathers is still alive.

From here I'm going to shift gears from the entitlement mentality and into other key issues. First up will be energy independence.

14

Energy Independence

This book is an extension of something I began on my website a few years ago as a fifty year plan. In attempting to emulate forward-thinking individuals like Newt Gingrich, I tried to project a long-term vision for America that didn't just seek to get votes in the next election and kick the proverbial can down the road. At some point, the buck had to stop and hard choices must be made.

Probably the worst omission I made in my thinking at the time was not taking into account the aspect of our nation's energy needs. However, back then the price of crude oil was still in the mid-double digits and gasoline could still be found for less than $3 per gallon, though the perfect storm which began to brew over the next year and eventually gave us two gasoline price spikes to $4 per gallon and beyond was beginning to take shape. Quickly I realized that addressing energy policy was necessary to make this a complete plan for adoption by others who love freedom and liberty.

The hitherto unknown aspects of $140 per barrel crude oil and correspondent gas prices back in 2008 set off a tidal wave of discontent with Congress, as Americans pleaded with their representatives in Washington to do something – anything – to stem the rising cost of energy. Unfortunately, those inside the Beltway created the problem for the most part and little could be accomplished when the most obvious solution was being blocked by the then-Speaker of the House and her majority party. Even when Republicans held a sit-in of sorts during that year's summer recess, the effort failed to sway any concerted effort to address the energy situation.

And by the time Election Day 2008 came, gas prices had

plummeted with the sharp, sudden downturn in the economy. Spiraling energy costs ceased to be an issue; instead, we elected a president who claimed energy prices would necessarily have to rise. Since then we've been on a roller coaster where gas prices seem to now oscillate between $3 and $4 per gallon.

In stating the those inside the Beltway created the problem, though, we need to do some review of history. Beginning in the early twentieth century, the fuel of choice for transport in America was oil in the form of gasoline, while heating oil was the ideal for keeping homes comfortable in the winter. Meanwhile, electricity was created through the use of coal, heated to provide the power to rotate the turbines which created the actual voltage cycling through the electrical lines.

Beginning in the 1960's, coal was joined by nuclear power and later natural gas became preferred as a home heating source. With the exception of nuclear power, which came from refining the element uranium, all of these sources for power and fuel for transport were carbon-based fossil fuels.

This balance of sources worked well until the early 1970's, when the first in a series of oil shocks plunged the nation into a recession and brought the price of gasoline into national focus. A generation who was used to seeing a gallon of gasoline sell for barely a quarter saw the price nearly double, seemingly overnight. In the late 1970's the price doubled again and suddenly the old style of gasoline pumps became obsolete because they weren't designed for an era when gasoline's per gallon price would exceed a dollar – the pumps only accounted for two-digit prices. The golden era of so-called muscle cars which thrived in the late '60's came to a screeching halt and econobox cars were introduced as quickly as Detroit could design and build them.

This sudden jarring change also showed that the then-Big Four American automakers needed to change and evolve; ironically it was American Motors – the automaker which already had the most small cars in its lineup – fading into insolvency. AMC's demise left the Big Three we're familiar with today. On the other hand, this period ushered in a slew of new Japanese imports that took the automotive market by storm because they were thrifty with gasoline.

On another front, air pollution also became a national concern. Starting in smog-choked southern California, the call was made to Congress to crack down on polluters. Eventually the auto industry was forced to clean up the output of its cars through the use of catalytic converters and the gasoline refiners no longer could use lead as an additive to boost the octane of their products. A decade later, the first standards for fuel efficiency were introduced, requiring automakers to maintain an increased corporate miles-per-gallon average. One loophole in CAFE standards eventually exploited by automakers was that trucks and utility vehicles were exempted, which led to the modern sport-utility vehicle.

Nor was nuclear power exempt from issues. Nuclear power plant development effectively ceased in America after the Three Mile Island debacle in 1979. The thought of a nuclear meltdown frightened the public – with some help from Hollywood, such as the movie "The China Syndrome" – and the question of what to do with nuclear waste also perplexed efforts to restart the process of building new plants. On top of that, the 1986 Chernobyl nuclear power plant accident in the Soviet Union turned America farther away from embracing nuclear power as a method of producing electricity. It wasn't until nearly a quarter-century past Chernobyl that President Obama paid lip service to the nuclear industry, proposing $8 billion in loan guarantees to jump-start the construction of two new nuclear plants. (As of this writing, construction is barely underway at one of the two projects, with completion slated for 2016.) And even that small renaissance is in doubt after the Fukushima nuclear disaster in Japan in 2011.

And the discussion of recent energy policy cannot be complete without mentioning the pressure placed on lawmakers to combat theorized anthropogenic global warming through the creation of energy via fossil fuels. While scientists in the 1970's fretted over whether our planet was entering a new Ice Age, by the time the next decade was over the more alarmist scientists in the climatology field were pleading the case that Earth was rapidly warming up. The hype reached its peak when former Vice-President Al Gore promoted the factually-challenged documentary "An Inconvenient Truth."

As we've found out over recent years though, a more inconvenient truth is that global temperatures have held steady or even dropped slightly since 1998. It's why the global warming phrase has now morphed into the more defensible "climate change." Unfortunately for them, as the scandal at East Anglia University in Great Britain has shown, junk scientists can no longer "hide the decline" by cooking the books and providing misleading information. It seemed as if the results were magically coming out the way the big money interests and government wanted them to – isn't that amazing when data which reflects the desired outcome like that occurs?

Those several paragraphs were just a quick overview of history. There's no way I could make this a short chapter if I documented each and every regulation and edict from inside the Beltway over the last few decades on how America's energy could be produced and used. Much of that red tape was created by the Environmental Protection Agency.

The EPA came into being under President Nixon in 1970, partly in response to a large oil spill off the California coast. Using the EPA as their weapon of choice, radical environmental groups slowly took away what had previously been *carte blanche* for energy companies to operate – no longer could power plants easily be built without a years-long approval process nor could oil companies explore for new product wherever they wished.

Instead, the mantra for radical environmentalists became one of conservation and "alternative" sources of energy such as wind power, solar energy, geothermal, and biofuels such as ethanol made from corn. In a easily ascertained game of unintended consequences, we've found that the ethanol mandates for which Al Gore as Vice-President cast the tie-breaking Senate vote have instead made America's grocery bills surge upward and caused food riots abroad because corn was in short supply. Obviously the price at the pump has gone through the roof and remains high despite the ethanol edicts and protectionism demanded by American farmers concerned about the prospect of importing less expensive and more efficient Brazilian ethanol created from sugar cane.

Worse, in 2007 the Supreme Court gave the EPA the power to regulate carbon dioxide. Obviously this ruling will allow a group of career bureaucrats who love nothing more than the power to regulate our way of life and enjoy the freedom of being unaccountable to voters the perfect device to make an end run around Congress and exert whatever misguided influence the cooked climate data has had on their world view. If you thought manufacturing was already dead in America, wait until the cap-and-trade legislation which stalled in Congress comes back as new regulation courtesy of the Environmental Protection Agency.

Over the next two generations America will begin to see a slow evolution from carbon-based fuels to those sources which occur naturally or are rapidly renewable. While the world will probably never completely run out of oil or natural gas, the cost to extract and transport it will someday become too prohibitive for the energy market to bear. But that day is decades, if not centuries, down the road. Between crude oil reserves that we've accounted for and other usable forms of oil which can be extracted, such as oil sands or oil shale, the world is set for awhile – even as global usage increases thanks to the emergence of China and India as developed nations.

However, this isn't a call to abandon the possibility of renewable energy. Instead, what I advocate is a solution which takes advantage of both the resources we have here at home and the ingenuity for which Americans are known.

The advantages of loosening restrictions on drilling and exploring for natural gas and oil are twofold. First of all, oil companies are always seeking to extract and transport their products as cheaply as possible. As it stands at the moment, the reason America imports so much of its oil can be very simply put: it's less expensive for oil companies to have the crude oil extracted in another country (for the most part that role is played by either Canada, Mexico, or Saudi Arabia) and transported here to be refined than it is to complete the entire process domestically. By eliminating the red tape, we bring the price advantage back to our own shores. While we'll likely never be totally self-sufficient again in oil production, we may be able to at least restrict our imports to those from North America, leaving the Middle East free to sell their oil to Europe and Asia and eliminating to some degree the ocean transport of crude oil.

The second advantage of producing more of our own oil is the sheer number of jobs which would be created. A new oil rig would employ dozens of workers in good-paying jobs and new refineries could each add hundreds more to that total. Factor in also the thousands of jobs which would need to be filled to construct both the physical plants and the infrastructure to connect these new wells and refineries to existing markets. Instead of taxing what those on the Left consider "windfall" profits and putting more pencil-pushers to work in Washington who determine which favored special interest will receive the federal dollars to pursue a blind alley in technology, why not allow the producers of oil and natural gas to spend the money where they see fit and create jobs that actually produce something? They're only the experts in the field!

But it's not all about producing and extracting oil and natural gas. We do have a place at the table for nuclear energy, provided that the utilities and companies manufacturing the components don't ask for huge subsidies in order to build them. (As I noted above though, President Obama created an $8 billion subsidy for just two new nuclear plants.) Again, much of the upfront cost to utilities comes from the maze of permitting and regulations which need to be completed before the first shovelful of dirt is ever turned on a site. It can lead us down the path to the day when the era of nuclear fission will end and the era of nuclear fusion to create energy will begin – the advantage of fusion is the elimination of radioactive waste products.

And future generations cannot completely ignore the idea of alternative energy – however, the huge subsidies and favored treatment these sources receive must be phased out, allowing the market to again dictate which approaches are best. All of these sources have benefits, but they vary from place to place – for example, a wind farm would work well out in the Great Plains or in certain offshore areas but other locales wouldn't be suited because the winds there remain too calm. The desert southwest may work well for solar panels, but mandating rooftop solar panels in damp, cloudy areas like the Pacific Northwest – not so good. Common sense can generally dictate where conditions are the most promising for these and other naturally occurring energy sources like geothermal and hydropower.

I cannot call this chapter complete, though, without bringing up another topic which needs to be broached – that of energy efficiency and conservation.

Many liberals and radical environmentalists will tell you that America can cut its dependence on foreign oil if we just took enough steps to conserve energy and accepted a few extra government mandates along the way. Barack Obama took that to its illogical conclusion during his otherwise successful Presidential campaign by suggesting that America wouldn't have to drill any new oil wells and could still maintain its energy needs with its current supply if Americans would simply drive with their tires properly inflated. It was the same rugged, can-do spirit that President Carter exhibited when he suggested keeping the thermostats lower during the winter and wearing an extra sweater to compensate. (Yes, that was sarcasm.)

One area many federal and state governmental bodies are choosing to tackle energy conservation by fiat is mandating new and renovated buildings comply with "green" standards. For the most part, their idea of a "green" building is one which complies with LEED certification.

Well, as I mentioned in Chapter 3, it just so happens that the writer of this very book has quite a bit of familiarity with LEED (which stands for Leadership in Energy and Environmental Design.) And while I applaud many of the energy efficiency steps which are an integral part of LEED, my biggest objection to the concept is the social engineering aspect. For example, LEED dictates that buildings must have a dedicated area for recycling, which is extra cost to the owner for little benefit to him. They also mandate that smoking either be prohibited in the completed building, or that expensive steps and tests are taken to ensure that tobacco smoke doesn't migrate from private spaces to public ones. These are just two examples of social engineering which has little impact on the amount of energy a building uses.

To me, these green building mandates like LEED certification are of dubious benefit to the overall aim of energy conservation and should be repealed. While it behooves an owner to choose wisely when considering the lighting, power, plumbing, and HVAC systems in a new or renovated structure, the first thing which needs to be looked at is the benefit of a more energy efficient system versus the cost. Personally, I believe a good payback period (the point where additional costs up front are eclipsed by the money saved) is five years or less. Most commonly available devices intended as energy savers come with such a short-term payback, while more esoteric ones take longer but still can be installed if the owner feels that the savings are worth the wait and the technology may be a selling point for a prospective client.

Over the next two generations, Americans will see vast changes in their daily lives. In my 47-plus years on the planet I've seen mankind walk on the moon, become tied to each other through wireless means (as I sit here writing this chapter on my laptop), and conquer a number of crippling or lethal diseases.

While putting a man on the moon was in the national interest, at least according to President Kennedy, and a task that government eventually solved, I don't believe the issue of energy independence needs a federal program or mandate from inside the Beltway to solve it. In fact, this is one area where I think there needs to be a push from the public to get government out of the way. It's already manifested itself in the clamor for more oil and natural gas drilling and promises to continue as Congress debates the issue further. As is normally the case, true leadership can be shown by allowing Americans to use their own judgment and common sense.

We all want to be able to have the energy we need to prosper available at the lowest possible price. It's time for our elected officials to stand aside and do nothing once they finish clearing the decks.

15

Veterans Affairs

The Cabinet-level Department of Veterans Affairs is a relatively recent creation, authorized by President Reagan in 1988. What I'm going to touch on in this chapter is more aligned with the direction and function of that Department than the actual global military strategy necessary for upcoming years. Some of that I'll discuss in my upcoming chapter about the Long War, better known to many as the "War on Terror" or simply Iraq and/or Afghanistan.

It's appropriate to bring this up in a book like mine because a large percentage of those who are political activists have served in our military, whether in peacetime or in a period of war like we're in now. Signs dotting the various TEA Party gatherings across the country pointed out that their bearers had served in Iraq or Afghanistan, Desert Storm, Vietnam, or even Korea and World War II. Obviously those who took the time to attend TEA Parties and other political events in order to make their feelings known see the direction this nation is going in and don't recognize it as the one they fought and watched their fellow soldiers die for.

Insofar as the rest of military strategy goes, I subscribe to the Reagan-era doctrine of "peace through strength" with an emphasis on forward deployment. This is why I'd advocated not completely retreating from Iraq or Afghanistan; alas, indications are we will be pretty much abandoning the gains we've made over the last decade in the name of political correctness.

By holding that opinion of advocating a forward force you could likely call me a neocon, but history doesn't bear that out. Since our earliest days our nation has defended itself well beyond its borders, beginning with battles against the Barbary pirates in and around the Mediterranean Sea. Over 200 years later we continue to find ourselves sailing our Navy and flying our Air Force over that body of water along with much of the rest of the globe.

The incident which originally placed this particular facet of veterans' affairs on my radar screen was the soap opera regarding conditions at the now-shuttered Walter Reed medical complex just outside Washington, D.C. Building 18 at that complex was described as a moldy, rat-infested firetrap of a structure, one which was already slated for closure and abandonment in a few years. But when news reports looked into the conditions wounded soldiers returning from Iraq were placed under by the continued use of Building 18, the story became yet another avenue for Congressional Democrats to maintain their mantra of "it's Bush's fault" each time problems occurred and needed to be addressed. Likewise, there are problems in the veterans' health care system – but they go far beyond the bricks and mortar of decrepit facilities and even beyond the lack of oversight and maintenance which placed Building 18 and others in the VA system in such atrocious condition. Like most Americans, I feel veterans deserve better.

In many areas of life, veterans get preferential treatment. This dates back to the days shortly after the Revolutionary War when pensions and land grants for war veterans were first established. Sponsored medical care for disabled veterans also dates back close to two centuries. Later, Congress began moving beyond the realm of financial and medical care and passed the original GI Bill at a time when World War II veterans were returning home from overseas and reestablishing their stateside lives.

The original GI Bill enabled qualifying veterans to buy homes and helped pave the way toward the postwar prosperity of the Fifties. Thousands of tract-home developments were created during this era, with reasonably-sized homes built for newly financially-empowered war survivors and their young families. It also firmly ensconced veterans as a class unto themselves when it came to receiving federal benefits.

As things stand now there are a great number of benefits to joining the military, including recruitment bonuses and help paying for college. Beyond service years, veterans remain eligible for federal assistance in job training, finding housing, preference in hiring for civil service work, and many other benefits not generally available to those who chose not to serve in the military. (Obviously there's a risk factor involved which makes dangling these perks to prospective recruits necessary.)

In most cases I don't have a problem with these perks because they actually benefit and supplement things available to the public at-large. Perhaps the costs of these particular veterans benefits need to have a closer eye placed on them in order to eliminate duplicity and assure that those who are receiving the benefits truly are entitled to them, but there's nothing stopping anyone who wants to train for a different career, buy a house, or apply for a civil service job whether they served in the military or not. On the other hand only veterans, their surviving spouses, and dependents are eligible for VA medical assistance. It's a more unique category that demands attention and is one where needed reforms are possible within a reasonable time frame. And time is of the essence as Vietnam veterans reach the end of their lifespan and those who served in Desert Storm become older and more afflicted with the diseases aging brings on.

I believe there's a solution which can help eliminate a lot of the government red tape that's bogged down the veterans' health care system and created situations which allowed problems like Building 18 to fester.

Health care should be about choices, and my plan seeks to allow current veterans their choice to the location where they'll be receiving their future health care needs. Many veterans (particularly the few World War II and Korean War vets remaining) would probably feel most comfortable with continuing to deal with the VA health care system as it is now. But I think newer veterans would jump at having a choice whether they wish to continue in the VA or be given vouchers by the federal government which can be used in one of two areas: payment for care at a hospital not affiliated with the VA when required, and/or establishing a Health Savings Account, with a high-deductible insurance policy through a qualified private insurer.

Meanwhile, future military personnel would simply be given the vouchers and allowed to choose for themselves the method and delivery of health care services.

Eventually this would lead to the closing of VA facilities, but what would likely happen is that existing non-VA facilities would begin to cater to the needs of the veteran population in an effort to secure their voucher dollars. It would eliminate a situation where services are (more or less) duplicated for two separate but co-mingled populations: the 60 million or so people eligible for VA services of some sort and the rest of us.

In coming years, we will begin to lose our Vietnam-era veterans, since most are already in their sixties and dealing with Social Security as well as the VA. They are being replaced by a Generation X of veterans who have a completely different set of needs and may chafe a little bit at the emphasis that the Department of Veterans Affairs places on older veterans. For example, the younger generation worries less about the effects of Agent Orange and more about their own particular set of health issues from fighting in a completely different kind of theater.

The GI Bill then returns in its full circle once again for the veterans of Iraq and Afghanistan as those who weren't seriously wounded in combat restore the emphasis back onto the educational and home purchasing aspects of the veterans' benefit package. Since these only supplement other programs for the public at large, this is a good time to reevaluate the entire spectrum of federal government involvement in the care and feeding of veterans.

Taking care of veterans through pensions, benefits, and the like is one of the few areas not specifically addressed in the Constitution where I feel the federal government indeed has a legitimate stake in regulating some of their day-to-day needs. It is because these men and women have sacrificed in service to our country that this is so. However, the idea of this chapter is to show that the

Washington should act as a supplement to the free market which exists for all the areas veterans have to deal with along with all the rest of us who didn't serve our nation in this manner, and not as the sole-source provider. A saying Rush Limbaugh made famous was that the purpose of the military is to "kill people and break things," so running a health care system doesn't meld well with their particular skill set.

By placing the decision in the hands of those who use it, eliminating the duplicity of two separate health care systems, and allowing the private sector to bring better competition to the veterans' health care market, it gives those who served their country an opportunity to select the treatment they feel is best for their needs, rather than the one-size-fits-all solution government bureaucracy seems to come up with.

In my next chapter I look at the conflict this generation of veterans is returning from, the ongoing skirmishes with loosely allied bands of Islamic terrorists I call the Long War.

16

The Long War

To begin this chapter, I think it bears repeating that we were warned at the start about the time the effort against Islamic fundamentalists would take. Noted President George W. Bush on September 20, 2001:

"This war will not be like the war against Iraq a decade ago, with a decisive liberation of territory and a swift conclusion. It will not look like the air war above Kosovo two years ago, where no ground troops were used and not a single American was lost in combat.

Our response involves far more than instant retaliation and isolated strikes. Americans should not expect one battle, but a lengthy campaign, unlike any other we have ever seen. It may include dramatic strikes, visible on TV, and covert operations, secret even in success."

Those words, spoken just nine days after the twin towers of the World Trade Center fell, began our offensive against terrorism with its twin fronts in Afghanistan and later Iraq. But Americans have seemed to forget that these words were spoken barely a decade ago; in fact, it only took seven years before the conventional wisdom that only a candidate tough on terror could be elected was belied by the 2008 Presidential election as economic issues took center stage.

We also seem to forget that several other countries outside the Middle East have felt the sting of radical Islamic terror in the last few years, with major events in Great Britain, Indonesia, France, and Spain, just to name a few. With the exception of the British, none of these countries had a significant number of combat personnel in Iraq or Afghanistan.

Although those on the left attempted originally to compare this effort against Islamic terror to the war in Vietnam – a war that was undertaken to stop the spread of Communism throughout southeast Asia – by its nature this war is totally different than the "Cold War" of my youth. However, the fear of nuclear annihilation is still present. Instead of the fallout shelters and drills of a bygone era that were to prepare us for a missile attack from the Soviet Union, the threat is now just as great of a so-called "suitcase nuke" or "dirty bomb" rendering a city uninhabitable and costing untold American lives. Additionally, China has demonstrated an ability to destroy satellites, which could be another tool terrorists engage eventually. With warm relations between China and Iran and Tehran's support of radical Islamic groups we're currently engaged with in Iraq, it's not difficult to imagine this technology becoming another weapon in the Islamic arsenal.

But Democrats seem to be in favor of diplomacy rather than solving this through the aggressive use of force. This shows most in our relationship with the theocracy in Iran, a religiously-based regime which has existed in a more or less pure form since the Shah was overthrown in 1979. In essence, the people of Iran traded one dictator for another, with the only difference being what basis laws were created in – now laws are based on interpretations of the Quran. Many of my readers probably recall the daily count of the number of days 52 Americans were held hostage after radical Islamists seized the American Embassy in Tehran. Not only did the situation spawn the long-running ABC News series "Nightline," it also helped seal the doom of President Carter's 1980 re-election chances. Most noteworthy about the eventual resolution of the crisis is that the hostages were released on the very day Carter's successor Ronald Reagan took over.

But the doves among us, mostly on the Democrat side, never seem to learn the lessons presented to them. Regarding the Iranian situation, one now infinitely more dangerous with that regime's pursuit of nuclear weapons, the liberals' mantra has remained one which declares, "Sanctions will work in Iran **if** we have the support of the international community."

I place the emphasis on "if" because, as was proven in the "Oil-For-Food" program and in the assistance Russia and China have given the Iranians in their war efforts, the so-called international community will cheat when they feel it's in their best interests to. Combine that with the stated tendency of radical Islamists – much like the Communists of a generation before – to extend one hand at the negotiating table while readying the knife in the other hand for that stab in the back, and it becomes clear in my eyes that the only way diplomacy works is when one side is completely subdued and has its terms of surrender dictated to them. America last enjoyed that sort of advantage at the end of World War II and eventually installed governments allied with our interests in Germany and Japan; in contrast the stalemate in Korea and defeat in Vietnam led to the establishment of unfriendly regimes in each region.

Most Americans are also blissfully unaware that there are two main and competing sects of Islam. I find it interesting that just 10 percent of Muslims subscribe to the Shi'ite sect, but that 10 percent are a majority in five nations. These five include both Iraq and Iran. If you study a bit further you'll find that the Salafists (or Wahhabists) consider themselves an even purer form of the majority Sunni sect. This is the brand of Islam practiced in Saudi Arabia and Qatar, and the one to which Osama bin Laden subscribed. Also, the Taliban in Afghanistan are another subsect of Sunnis. In essence, our fight against radical Islam is against a small portion of the entire Islamic world – however, that small portion tends to congregate in countries which are some of the leaders against us in the Long War.

Because of this factor we will likely be fighting these enemies for quite a spell; thus a difficult question arises as to what sort of help we can get. We need to identify and support Islamic nations that are more moderate to help in this battle – part of the reason we were in Iraq and Afghanistan was the effort to install leadership more friendly to our interests. Other countries such as Bahrain, Turkey, and Kuwait have also been helpful in providing forward bases for us to work from.

It's here that I depart from many in the conservative movement, and especially part ways with those in the isolationist camp which makes up a significant percentage of TEA Partiers.

Part of our reinvention is facing the fact that we are the source of freedom for the globe and a healthy chunk of the world economy. Thus, our national interests transcend our borders and isolationism cannot succeed in the world today. While we do need to secure our borders better and work on free but fair trade, we also need to realize that having American troops in far-flung places on the globe is going to be a fact for the foreseeable future. It's one thing that our Founders may not have thought of in their era.

For example, George Washington opined in his Farewell Address:

"The great rule of conduct for us in regard to foreign nations is, in extending our commercial relations to have with them as little political connection as possible. So far as we have already formed engagements let them be fulfilled with perfect good faith. Here let us stop.

Europe has a set of primary interests which to us have none or a very remote relation. Hence she must be engaged in frequent controversies, the causes of which are essentially foreign to our concerns. Hence, therefore, it must be unwise in us to implicate ourselves by artificial ties in the ordinary vicissitudes of her politics or the ordinary combinations and collisions of her friendships or enmities.

Our detached and distant situation invites and enables us to pursue a different course. If we remain one people, under an efficient government, the period is not far off when we may defy material injury from external annoyance; when we may take such an attitude as will cause the neutrality we may at any time resolve upon to be scrupulously respected; when belligerent nations, under the impossibility of making acquisitions upon us, will not lightly hazard the giving us provocation; when we may choose peace or war, as our interest, guided by justice, shall counsel.

Why forgo the advantages of so peculiar a situation? Why quit our own to stand upon foreign ground? Why, by interweaving our destiny with that of any part of Europe, entangle our peace and prosperity in the toils of European ambition, rivalship, interest, humor, or caprice?

It is our true policy to steer clear of permanent alliances with any portion of the foreign world, so far, I mean, as we are now at liberty to do it, for let me not be understood as capable of patronizing infidelity to existing engagements. I hold the maxim no less applicable to public than to private affairs that honesty is always the best policy. I repeat, therefore, let those engagements be observed in their genuine sense. But in my opinion it is unnecessary and would be unwise to extend them."

But he then stated:

"Taking care always to keep ourselves by suitable establishments on a respectable defensive posture, we may safely trust to temporary alliances for extraordinary emergencies."

Where I differ with our first President solely lies in the fact that we are not in a "detached and distant situation" anymore. As I spoke of earlier, our interests are now global and our foreign policy must reflect this fact. To this end, we must do whatever it takes and resort to whichever "temporary alliances" are needed to subdue the threat posed by radical Islam.

I do have one other main point to make. Some are of the opinion that we need to pull out of the United Nations, and I tend to agree with them.

By its nature the UN is populated with all nations, regardless of their devotion to the freedom of their citizens. A tyrannical nation like China has an equal say and veto power there as we do, therefore I believe it's truly not in our best interest to be fully invested in such an organization. Add in its bloated and relatively corrupt bureaucracy saddled by inertia and the benefits from divesting ourselves from the UN grow. Using the Hussein regime in Iraq as an example, we found the UN did nothing to a tyrant who violated seventeen UN resolutions until we took it upon ourselves to build a coalition to take care of the problem, which we solved. Truly we have a better solution in "going it alone" if we must when the alternative is begging for a hall pass from the international community.

Another piece necessary for success will be a hands-off approach by Congress. History shows that their meddling has made for disastrous results, like that which occurred in Vietnam.

In June 1970 the Senate passed a resolution regarding the Vietnam war. This resolution, known as the Cooper-Church Amendment, ended funding for U.S. troops and advisers in Cambodia and Laos, banned combat operations over Cambodian airspace to support Cambodian forces without prior Congressional approval, and cut funding to support South Vietnamese forces stationed outside of Vietnam. It seemed harmless enough because it would have no real effect on American troops fighting within Vietnam. In fact, the original bill died because of a veto threat, only to have a slightly modified measure pass a lame-duck Congress that December.

But Cooper-Church opened the door, and once the GOP was blown out in the 1974 elections, Democrats felt free to cut off funding for the war entirely. We all now know what tragedies awaited the people of Southeast Asia in the years immediately after our shameful withdrawal. After Saigon fell, certainly veterans of the conflicts and their supporters stateside had to wonder whether the lives of friends and fellow servicemen lost in Southeast Asia were sacrificed in vain.

Once again, we face an enemy that does not deal fairly at the diplomatic table. A broadly accepted interpretation of the Quran reveals that lying and deceit are acceptable tactics in the effort to spread Islam globally, and sacrifice of one's self is considered noble as a shortcut to Paradise. Thus, the only way we can defeat this sort of enemy is to wipe them out in whatever manner necessary to demoralize them into surrender. Words will not do it, but in my mind military action has some chance of success. To that end, Americans have to remain diligent and determined to succeed.

Fortunately, we haven't had to militarize our border, but we do have an issue which requires addressing. It's the subject of my next chapter.

17

Border Security and Immigration

Some have estimated that there are up to 20 million illegal immigrants in America. Most are from Mexico and Central America but a few come from other places around the globe, including countries which are on America's terrorist watch list. Their impact is obvious – just look at the bilingual store signage many national merchants now feature. Even where I live, in a city situated over 1,000 miles from the Mexican border, we have Spanish-language radio stations in our area. All of this was unheard of in most parts of America outside places like New York or Los Angeles even 10 years ago.

However, this immigration spigot along our southern border had been dripping for most of the last fifty years. It's only become a rushing torrent in the last decade as Mexican and Central American economies stagnated; meanwhile America's abundant thirst for cheap labor combined with easy access to free health care and the chance for children of these undocumented workers to become American citizens by virtue solely of being born within our borders (the so-called "anchor babies") enabled this problem to become a hot-button issue – so hot that a heretofore obscure Congressman from Colorado, Tom Tancredo, made a name for himself as a border hawk and became one of the second-tier GOP candidates for President in 2008. Before there were TEA Parties, many of the participants agreed with Tancredo that America needed to take a harder line on illegal immigration. On the other hand, Texas governor and 2012 Presidential candidate Rick Perry quickly lost traction in his campaign after people found out more about the in-state tuition for illegal aliens he supported early on as governor.

For most of the late 19th and early 20th century, America was the land of opportunity for immigrants of all stripes. Wave after wave of Germans, Poles, Irish, Italians, Greeks, Asians, and others from all points of the globe converged on America and filled up this land from sea to shining sea. My ancestors, mostly from Germany but with a few Poles mixed in, were in that group. All of them had to deal with the language barrier and some amount of discrimination – as in the mid-19th century "No Irish Need Apply" signs – but if they didn't adapt, their children surely did because they wanted to become Americans. Most cities of the era had enclaves where these immigrants eventually settled to be with those whom they shared language and culture with. But even moreso than the fun poked at rural Americans today, people from the "old country" were looked down upon by the next generation and those immigrants' children who were born or raised in America grew somewhat ashamed of their cultural roots, leaving behind these old-world enclaves to live out their American dreams.

Eventually the pendulum started swinging the other way and in the last half-century or so Americans have once again embraced their ancestry through vacations to the homeland, ethnic festivals, and the like. As a native of a Rust Belt city, I recall summers there being punctuated by weekend gatherings celebrating Irish, Polish, German, Mexican, Hungarian, and Greek food, dance, and culture. (And those featured some good eating, let me tell you – particularly the Polish Festival. There you can get REAL kielbasa, and not the bland mass-produced sausage those outside the Polish community call kielbasa.)

On the other hand, when you look at this new wave of immigrants, who mainly hail from Mexico and Central America, the large majority of them have played the role of eventual assimilation in reverse by demanding America adapt to their culture and language instead of desiring to join the proverbial "melting pot" of Americans like immigrants of yore.

Worse yet, the influx of illegal immigrants has overwhelmed border states, especially California, which lack the resources in either the public or private sector to accommodate those crossing the border. Hardest hit in that region of the country are schools which have to account for children who need additional classroom time to learn English and hospitals which either have closed emergency rooms or folded outright because of the uncompensated care federal law demanded they give to the swarms of illegal immigrants who arrived needing their services. Demand there is especially high for obstetric services as pregnant women close to term try to make it across the border in order to give birth in America, knowing those anchor babies are automatically granted citizenship simply by virtue of their birth here.

And while most undocumented workers are simply job-seekers who can't find employment in their home country, large numbers of them also contribute to the rampant crime plaguing some sections of the country. The state of California has estimated that one out of four of their prison inmates are in the country illegally, and street gangs (most famously the MS-13 gang) comprised mainly of illegal immigrants wreak havoc on cities throughout the nation. They also have made the prisons themselves part of the war zone.

While these foreign workers generally don't make high wages, they still have economic punch. With that economic impact and the desire of major corporations to be politically correct – lest they offend some legal organization someplace enough to incite a lawsuit – these businesses are bending over backwards in an effort to appease the undocumented folks streaming in across our southern border. An early example was Bank of America, which eliminated the requirement of a Social Security number for California applicants to receive a credit card.

But in America things always come around to politics, and eventually this long-festering situation led to a fight among two groups of Republicans. This battle pitted the Chamber of Commerce types who liked the idea of an inexpensive labor pool to do "those jobs Americans won't do" against the border and security hawks who saw danger in the flood of humanity crossing the border, knowing that there were some among them who wish our nation ill.

In choosing sides, I stand with the border and security hawks.

A sad fact about our current situation is there simply hasn't been enough intestinal fortitude to get serious about border security. For several years before leaving Congress after an unsuccessful 2008 Presidential bid, California Congressman Duncan Hunter tirelessly worked to secure funding for improving the fence along our Mexican border. Despite finally winning the funding to get this done in 2006, by the time he retired from Congress only a small segment of the hundreds of miles of improved fencing necessary had been built. Most of the rest had become bogged down by environmental concerns, squabbles over eminent domain issues, and, most of all, a lack of will to get the job done by the pro-immigration Bush and Obama Administrations.

The "virtual" fence was supposed to be finished by 2009, but now is in limbo and will drag out well beyond a 2016 completion date – that is, if Congress continues to allocate money into its construction and the contractors can solve problems with the portions already designed and built. The aforementioned Rick Perry is even skeptical a fence would work, which shows how difficult it is to get Republicans to agree on the need – let alone Democrats, who tend to advocate open borders.

Even where a sound fence exists, our Border Patrol doesn't just deal with illegal immigrants who are crossing to get work but also with the "coyotes" who shepherd them across the border and, more dangerously, well-armed drug traffickers who have enough financial clout to bribe and corrupt the authorities on the Mexican side of the border, leaving our Border Patrol as the only line of defense. Sadly, the battle narcotraffickers wage with the Mexican authorities sometimes spills over to the American side of the border, with deadly results.

More troubling for border security is the political football created by overzealous efforts to enact gun control. The Gunwalker scandal, better known as Operation Fast and Furious, led to the death of a Border Patrol agent. Guns which were supposed to be tracked instead found their way to Mexican drug cartels and promptly disappeared off our radar screen until Border Patrol Agent Brian Terry was murdered in a 2010 shootout with drug smugglers, with the gun used being traced back to the operation. The political stakes got even higher when Attorney General Eric Holder was found in contempt of Congress over his refusal to cooperate with a House investigation into Operation Fast and Furious.

Another complication for immigration officials occurs far from our borders, and involves many who came here legally. A 2008 report by the Center for Immigration Studies documented that over half of those here illegally arrived in the United States via a legal visa but either obtained that visa under false pretenses (such as arriving on a tourist visa but instead securing work) or remained in the United States after the visa's expiration date – many were guilty on both counts.

Perhaps the most famous cases of overstaying visas involved President Obama's relatives – while the news about his half-aunt Zeituni Onyongo being here illegally became public days before the 2008 election it didn't affect the outcome. Half-uncle Omar Okech Obama also made news by being arrested for a DUI offense in Massachusetts, when it was learned he had a pending deportation order from 1992.

Congress has made several attempts to increase the number of foreign workers allowed but their tendency has been to prefer allowing in those workers who are skilled or semi-skilled as opposed to manual laborers – which leads me to the other side of the coin.

The solution of putting up a stronger security fence and enabling our Border Patrol to become a quasi-military outfit in order to fight against the heavily armed drug and human smugglers who operate along what's best described as a lawless Mexican border is just a small bite out of the whole enchilada. The other end of the illegal immigration chain is the employer side, where we also need to crack down on those employers who knowingly hire illegal aliens. Obviously this piece of the overall strategy is going to upset the Chamber of Commerce types, but there's thousands out there who've knowingly or unknowingly had their Social Security number hijacked by someone who's using it to work here illegally.

One step undertaken by the federal government and bitterly fought by the Chamber of Commerce is a program called E-Verify, a federal database employers can use to quickly find out whether a potential employee's Social Security information checked out as legal. E-Verify has survived several attempts to kill it, so opponents now are using the tenuous claim of inaccuracy to discourage employers from using it. Despite those claims of inaccuracy, several states have mandated E-Verify for contractors doing business with state government.

There's another question which needs to be asked, too, one which addresses our neighbor to the south. It's unfortunate that the Mexican economy has put itself in such a bad state that emigration by a large chunk of their young male population is deemed necessary, particularly when one considers all of the oil they sell to us. Why can't they support their own people with decent industrial jobs? It was a phenomenon not lost on outgoing Mexican President Felipe Calderon, who even questioned whether his relatives are working in the United States legally. Speaking to the immigration issue from Mexico's perspective, he was quoted in 2008 in the Washington *Times*, "We want (those who emigrated to the U.S.) to come back; we want them to find jobs here in Mexico." Continued President Calderon, "We miss them. These are our best people. These are bold people, they're young, they're strong, they're talented." As talented as they may be, the lure of a better way of life in the United States continues to be a magnet for Mexican residents.

In short, these are three legs of the border security and immigration stool: tighter physical security at the border with a stronger show of force against drug and human trafficking, a better program to ensure those in the country on a visa do not overstay their allowed period, and a crackdown on employers who don't show due diligence in checking whether a worker has the proper status to be in the country.

However, the solution isn't complete with simple border security upgrades and immigration reform, for there are other needs which have to be addressed.

Another simple step is to make English our official language of government. Additionally, it's my belief that bilingual education needs to be scrapped. Just like the immigrants in the days of old, the adults may feel more comfortable to converse in their native tongue but in order for children to advance in our society they need to learn English as their first language. There's absolutely nothing wrong with being multilingual but in America the vast majority of people still speak English as their first and only language; moreover, if English becomes the official language of government immigrants will need to have some mastery of it to become citizens. If one were to move to Japan it would be expected that this individual learn enough of the language to get by and their children would be taught Japanese as their first language. So it should be with the English language in America.

If America is to survive and have a chance to enact the entirety of my body of ideas, among other things it has to curb this slide into multiculturalism.

By Balkanizing our culture in the way we have over the last quarter-century, we're isolating pockets in our country that do not speak the language and have no desire to become Americans, at the expense of millions who dream about coming to America and becoming just like us through hard work and ingenuity. There are thousands of businesses owned by immigrants who did just that through legal means, and the focus on illegal immigrants undeservedly tars them with the same brush. Misguided federal policies have turned the heat off from under our melting pot, and one task we have in the coming decades is to revitalize the process by which those who want to come to our nation can become Americans.

Among the duties naturalized citizens adopt in coming here, perhaps the most coveted is the right to vote for their leaders. That's what I cover with my next chapter.

18

Election Reform

2008 marked a watershed year in American electoral politics. Before much of the country had even put away its holiday decorations from 2007, party regulars in Iowa gathered to begin the selection process for a President who wouldn't even win election for over ten months and wouldn't be sworn in until the early days of 2009. And while much of the action in the previous Presidential election cycle commenced in March of 2004, by that same calendar point in 2008 the GOP nomination had already been decided for John McCain while Barack Obama had a secure lead over Hillary Clinton for the Democrats' nod. Meanwhile, when Maryland Congressman Wayne Gilchrest lost in his party's primary on February 12 of that year, it assured him of a record 10-plus month status as a lame duck – barely 15 months after many of those very same voters returned him to office in November, 2006. I'm going to address this piece of the electoral pie as part of my overall call for reform, but there are other slices I think merit attention first.

The very first thing which needs to occur is to require a photo ID to vote at the ballot box, or have one on file with a signature card for absentee ballots. It just makes sense to me that, in a society where I'm asked for my ID in order to place money into my own bank account, some form of photo identification needs to be required to exercise one of our most precious rights.

Normally the left-wingers scream about this point, contending that requiring ID disenfranchises the poor. One test case was the state of Georgia, who made the proposal and addressed initial concerns about shutting out poor and minority voters who couldn't afford the few dollars involved in securing a state-issued photo identification by offering to pony up a few hundred thousand dollars to allow anyone who could get to their DMV their own photo identity card. But that still wasn't good enough for the naysayers on the Left. I guess then I have to ask what they're so afraid of? Are they worried that their ideas aren't good enough to appeal to a majority of those who vote? (I know if I were them I would be; however, they do have a fairly compliant media on their side as I'll discuss in Chapter 21.)

Thus, if we adopt part number one above we'll have a state-issued photo identification card which can be used at the polls to verify that a voter is who he or she claims to be. Otherwise, they'll fill out a provisional ballot and then it would be up to the local Board of Elections to decide whether the vote was cast legally.

The next step is to use the newest computer technology to process the votes and allow easy counting, but have a backup paper trail set up as a double-check. Conspiracy theories about the 2000 and 2004 elections aside, and using my bank as an example again, every time I put in or take out money I get a receipt. Something tells me that voting can easily be the same way, and with the paper backup no one in the tinfoil hat brigade can claim a Diebold conspiracy as they did in those two elections that President Bush won. Does anyone else find it strange that none of these conspiracy theories are ever brought up when Democrats like Barack Obama win?

With these first two steps I've taken care of making sure the people who are eligible to vote can do so (once) and that their votes would be accounted for properly. However, there are two other items many states have enacted which, in my opinion, need to be rolled back.

First of all, as of this writing over thirty states have provisions for early voting, with some even allowing same-day registration. While most states restrict their early voting to a selected number of locations, there's still the concern about securing the ballots for the extra days as well as adequate staffing for those additional hours the polls are open. Moreover, while the evidence is somewhat anecdotal, the wait times claimed for voting on early voting days can discourage people from exercising their franchise if they indeed cannot vote on Election Day for some reason.

I believe that we have adequate means of voting in place without the additional days being necessary. Between the polling places being open for a lengthy time on Election Day (usually polls are open from 6:30 or 7 in the morning until 7:30 or 8 at night, depending on state law) and the option of absentee balloting, my contention is that the number of voters who actually wish to participate in the process have a fair chance of doing so. With these two voting methods already in place, there's no need to extend the potential for voter fraud and tampering by adding several days to the process. Similarly, I don't believe voting by mail or through the internet will enhance turnout all that much, but instead open the door for rampant gaming of the system.

Regarding absentee balloting, I further believe there should be some restrictions placed back on the practice. I don't really care for what I call "shall-issue" rules – that is, not having a legitimate cause for needing an absentee ballot but wanting one "just because." While many states have this type of approach as a means of encouraging turnout, I object because this method leaves some opening for a lack of accountability.

A more common-sense approach would be one where certain classes of people remain eligible without needing an additional excuse (such as those over 60 years of age, physically disabled, or serving in the military and stationed out of the state), but a qualified reason for voting absentee has to be provided for others. Personally I've voted absentee only about a half-dozen times in my life – mostly while I was in college, but in 2004 I voted absentee for Ohio because I found out I'd moved to Maryland too late to be registered there for the November election. Happenstances in life like those are legitimate reasons to get an absentee ballot, whereas wanting one just because you don't want to drive to the polling place on Election Day is not.

Perhaps it simply falls into the category of overzealousness, but this is a true story. On the weekend before the 1996 election I was laid up in the hospital with pneumonia but I'll have been damned if I wasn't going to be out for Election Day – even if I had to check myself out – to at least vote for Bob Dole (read: against Bill Clinton) if I couldn't work the polls. If there were a reason to need an absentee ballot, this would have been one but as I recall it has to be requested for in advance. You couldn't just go to the Board of Elections and ask for an absentee ballot on the day of the election. As it turned out I recovered enough to be let out on the Sunday before the election and voted in my regular manner, but this brings up the point that there are legitimate reasons to need an absentee ballot which come up at the last minute. We as a society, though, have abused the privilege.

Most of you are familiar with the term "money talks and bullshit walks." This term is doubly true in the political world, and both state and national election laws now feature restrictions on candidate financing. When the McCain-Feingold reforms for federal campaigns (Congressional and Presidential elections) were passed in 2003, they were supposed to take the money out of politics – but the 2008 Presidential election saw the spending total surpass $1 billion. Over $600 million of that cash was spent by Barack Obama, who reneged on an earlier pledge to accept public funding for the general election and outspent John McCain by about a 5:1 margin overall. Furthermore, the toll for contested Senatorial races generally reached $10 million or more while competitive Congressional seats generally saw spending in the seven-figure range.

Naysayers have predicted that the *Citizens United v. Federal Election Commission* decision by the Supreme Court will open the spigots to even more money in politics, as corporations and unions had restrictions removed on their giving to campaigns. While conservatives simply called it leveling the playing field since unions had previously enjoyed fewer limits than corporations had, Congressional Democrats vowed to enact legislation putting the caps on corporate giving back into effect. It's an issue which had impact on the 2010 Congressional elections and remains squarely in the crosshairs for 2012.

And while the McCain-Feingold regulations failed in their advertised promise to get money out of politics, other devious changes which came along with the bill's passage gave it the reputation of an "incumbent protection act" as restrictions were placed on advertising within 60 days of an election. (This also was overturned in the *Citizens United* decision.) Perhaps it's ironic that the co-author of this Senate bill was defeated in his Presidential bid, in part because of his own restraints.

Personally I think any and all contribution limits should be abolished and the process freed up as much as practical for American citizens. (Contributions by foreign nationals are and should remain a no-no.) But with that carrot comes the stick of daily and accessibly reporting any and all contributions to a particular campaign. So if AFSCME gives $50 million to Barack Obama's re-election campaign, within 24 hours anyone in the pajamas media can say, hey, AFSCME members, look what your union dues are paying for. If the trial lawyers' association gives $20 million to Obama, we can immediately follow the money and ask what the *quid pro quo* is there? Obviously the situation holds true as well if the national Chamber of Commerce gives $15 million to Mitt Romney.

But, one may argue, wouldn't that make the little guy's $25 contribution to a Presidential candidate meaningless? After all, it's also said that money talks and more money talks louder. Perhaps this is true but the people still hold the absolute power of the vote. Too, if I've found out that someone or some political action committee donated to a candidate or cause I don't support, I can choose to act accordingly. For example, when I get the annual reports from companies I invest in, I check and see who their board members make political donations to and withhold share votes from those candidates who support people I don't feel are friendly to the goals of the business as I see them. If more people did that, the situation would police itself.

After all, George Soros donated many of his millions toward various entities advocating the defeat of President Bush back in 2004, but he only had one actual vote in the matter. I'll grant he influenced many to follow him and vote against Bush, but others worked and donated to the Bush side and the President prevailed because he and his supporters convinced 59 million people to vote for him. In 2008 the financial backing was much the same behind President Obama but not so much on the GOP side, thus the results were different.

Now to the question of primaries being pushed back earlier and earlier. To me, it's insane that we've already dragged this election process out to a length bordering on the ridiculous and if the trend continues we'll be starting the actual voting and caucusing for the 2016 Presidential election around Election Day of 2015 – although we had some rule changes put into effect for 2012 which dampened this a little bit by making delegate allocation in early primaries proportional instead of winner-take-all. Still, the Iowa caucuses were held early in January as they were in 2008.

In this instance my adopted home state of Maryland had plenty to be proud of in the way it runs state elections, as did a number of others with similar state election calendars. Sadly, a federal law change ended Maryland's practice of holding their gubernatorial primary on the second Tuesday of September, a date which fell 8 weeks before the general election, with the filing deadline occurring in early July. This was timing that gave all of the candidates and their public the maximum amount of time to get together and interact so the public could make an informed choice with as many candidates in the running as possible.

But Maryland (and other states with early-September primaries) ran afoul of a noble federal law change which allowed soldiers overseas ample time to receive and return a ballot, so in 2011 Maryland changed its gubernatorial primary election (held in the even-numbered years not involving a Presidential election) to a date in June. I'd have preferred August, but late June isn't too bad considering some states hold their primaries much earlier in the year.

Conversely, in the runup to the 2008 Presidential election we knew who the two leading candidates were a full eight months beforehand. In 2004 there was some case of "buyer's regret" among Democrats that summer when John Kerry didn't turn out to quite be the candidate they thought they'd get in the spring when the race was essentially decided – the same held true for conservative Republicans in 2008 who were dissatisfied with John McCain. As history showed, much of 2008 was consigned to mudslinging and negative campaigning between the Republicans and Democrats and little positive was done in Congress because no one wanted to hurt their chances at re-election. (Instead, they handed out federal bailout money like candy at Halloween, with the Wall Street banks and United Auto Workers union at the front of the line.)

I think I have a better idea for the next Presidential cycle – it's time to get back to sanity. Of course, Presidential politics are dictated in large part by the obvious fact Election Day comes in November, but the party nominating conventions also play a role. Traditionally they had taken place in July and August, but now they are scheduled around Labor Day. It's a step in the right direction, but I'd like them to be even later in the process.

If we move the conventions even later on the calendar, to mid-September, they commence at a point people begin to pay attention to the campaigns anyway. One party can start its national convention the Monday after Labor Day and the other one the following Monday, alternating between cycles. There would be plenty of time remaining to have the Presidential and Vice-Presidential debates. (As an aside, I'd like to see those debates every two weeks, but with a 60 minute time frame and devoted to a single topic, such as one on the economy, one on foreign policy, one on energy-related items, and so on. The topics could easily be picked via polling data and other similar means.)

So now we work backwards from those mid-September conventions with the selection of primary dates. A schedule I've always thought would be a good idea would be to have a series of regional primaries held on consecutive weeks. Six regions of eight states each would hold primaries, and they would begin with the Tuesday after July 4th and end in August. That's plenty of time for convention delegates to make the plans required to attend their respective gatherings. Naturally, to assure each area would get the "prime" first spot once every six cycles, the regions would run elections in a particular predetermined order, the first one in a given cycle sliding back to last in the next cycle.

Using my adopted home state as an example, the idea Maryland tried to promote in 2008 of having a "regional" primary date with the District of Columbia and Virginia would be realized, just on a larger scale. For example, Maryland voters could be teamed up with those in Delaware, Virginia, the District of Columbia, West Virginia, the Carolinas, and Pennsylvania with our own regional primary.

I'd even allow Iowa and New Hampshire to be exempt and continue with their influential first caucus and primary, but these could be moved back into late June.

So instead of having this process last almost a year, my proposal compresses it into five months. This gives the American people, who are showing a shorter and shorter attention span, a much brisker and better focused campaign for our highest office and also means Congress can get more done (or undone, in some instances) because they wouldn't have to worry quite as much about influencing the Presidential race. Perhaps Congress could simply adjourn for their Labor Day recess and not return until after the election for a short lame-duck session – that is if they could ever get their fiscal duty of authorizing the next year's budget finished before Labor Day.

I happen to believe voting is the most important civic duty most of us do over the course of a year. I'm writing this with the earnest belief that these reforms would go a long way to increasing the percentage of people who actually exercise their right as citizens to vote, and, better yet, make the process one where more well-informed people become serious about the choices they make for our nation's leadership.

19

Race Relations

This is another chapter I didn't include in the blog posts which were the kernel of this book. But part of the reason for its inclusion now is because the target audience is arguably the most colorblind generation in history. For proof, one only needs to acknowledge the election of a man of color, Barack Obama, to the presidency and the sheer number of those under 30 who voted for him, as about 2/3 of the 18-to-25 vote went Obama's way. (While Barack Obama is considered the first black President, in reality his parentage is half-white, 3/8 Arabic, and only 1/8 black. Regardless, he indeed doesn't look like any of the Presidents on our dollar bills.)

A criticism of TEA Parties often delivered from the Left is that they're simply a gathering of angry white men and women who are only upset because a black man is now President of the United States. Where were these protests when President Bush was telling us that we had to destroy the free market in order to save it, they ask?

There are a lot of us who were upset about that decision, though, and President Bush's handling of the economic downturn was one of the major factors in John McCain's eventual defeat. As for the racial makeup of the TEA Party movement itself, the number of minority participants is growing as they look past President Obama's race and question his policy decisions.

While the leaps and bounds we have made from Martin Luther King's speech in which he referred to a dream of a society based on the content of one's character are clearly evident, the reality is that far too many governmental affairs continue to be dictated by the amount of pigment one naturally has. Having began the practice of affirmative action during King's lifetime – mainly with the Great Society proposed by President Lyndon Johnson – we're approaching a half-century of racial preferences encoded into the laws of the land.

There have been efforts to fight back in the last decade or so, with a handful of states approving ballot measures eliminating the practice of affirmative action in certain areas, such as college admissions. In many of these cases, however, the opposition who wants to maintain their race-based fiefdoms simply finds a friendly state court who nullifies the will of the voters and returns the practice to the *status quo*. California is one state notorious for that practice.

Consider as well that in the same 2008 election where Obama was elected the issue of race-based preference was on the ballot in Colorado and Nebraska; while Nebraska passed their ballot issue easily, the Colorado version narrowly failed. However, Colorado voters faced a large number of proposals on their ballot and may have lumped some of the more egregious attempts at government by referendum with the affirmative action issue, perhaps explaining one of the few ballot failures that pro-colorblind society issues have had.

Furthermore, while race was the original basis for the practice of affirmative action in hiring and set-asides for publicly-funded projects, color-based selection has expanded and morphed into the area of gender and in the near-term future threatens to include the behavioral-based selection by sexual preference. In many instances, gay rights activists compare their current efforts to those Dr. King and many others undertook 50 years or so ago, but miss a key point – where one has a choice in which gender they seek to sleep with (or, to use another example, their religious faith), they seldom can be one color and pass for another.

Another quirk in the preference system is the influx of Hispanic immigrants into our society. With Latinos now becoming the largest minority group, the question becomes where they'll fit into the whole race-based system because many lighter-skinned

Hispanics can pass for white. However, the immigrants face a barrier unto their own because most speak Spanish as their native tongue, and the next step for affirmative action activists may be to include language as another set-aside. With that, the cycle will merrily move on unless we make a push to stop the madness.

The idea of affirmative action has broken down over the decades because it's become a quota-based system. Set-asides are a prime example of this; most states dictate that a certain percentage of their overall contract work be awarded to companies that are either minority- or woman-owned. And while this hand up served a purpose early on, unscrupulous companies quickly figured out that putting a minority or female figurehead at the top was an easy way to skirt the competition and unfairly grab a share of lucrative state and federal contracts, by which they defeated the original purpose. In the meantime, companies owned by those who weren't favored by the preferences were placed at a competitive disadvantage – in particular this affected start-up companies who weren't in the existing "good old boy" network already in place for the remaining portion of the contracts not dictated by set-asides. In turn, those companies who benefited from the laws became a network unto themselves and are a major part of the lobby which seeks to keep set-asides in place.

The problem with quotas as a whole is that ability is not distributed equally among all. To use an extreme example, if NBA or NFL teams suddenly had to "reflect the society they exist in" a number of players who have shown themselves to possess excellence in the skills required to play the sport at the highest level would suddenly find themselves out of a job, while a less accomplished player of another race (or gender) would take his place. We even have a case study of this where the NBA is concerned; witness the relative popularity and revenue taken in by the average NBA team compared to that of even a championship WNBA team. While most casual sports fans can tell you the reigning NBA champions are the Miami Heat, it's only a hardcore basketball fan who could recall the WNBA champions. (For the record, the Minnesota Lynx won the 2011 WNBA crown in a three-game sweep of the Atlanta Dream.)

While I used a fairly extreme but obvious example, we can translate a lesser version of this to many other areas of life. Some of the most prominent colleges and universities have maintained a complex and tacit quota-based selection process in selecting students for admission, granting extra credit to students who come from a minority background. Unfortunately, a larger than average number of these students so admitted don't succeed in the setting for various reasons.

In many cases it's simply a lack of the ability needed to prosper at the highest level that sets up a minority applicant for failure in that extremely competitive environment. Unfortunately, this failure further damages the cause for a colorblind society, whereas had the student been rejected by the elite school they may have found a better fit at a school considered just a shade below the elite institutions. Meanwhile a more-qualified potential student may be denied the opportunity for his or her full potential to shine through simply because he or she was born with light skin. (Let's face it – the quotas generally are set up to increase the number of black students who attend these prominent schools.)

In America, the ideal our Founding Fathers sought was the equality of opportunity. As I stated back at the beginning of this chapter, the Millennial Generation (those born in the last thirty years) is likely the most colorblind we've had, so now is a perfect time to begin erasing the stereotypes which have been perpetuated by affirmative action and set-asides, the ones where people question the ability of those whose skin color or gender places them in the groups who have benefited in the past from those practices.

The first obvious solution to the problem would be to gradually phase out and sunset practices which favor a minority or particular gender. While this could be done overnight, in practice incrementalism was how we were saddled with affirmative action. Perhaps, then, the best strategy would be to achieve the reverse in the same manner but at an accelerated pace. It also gives a chance for firms who have benefited from the practice to strengthen themselves as the competition becomes more fierce – no longer would they be sheltered by laws inhibiting the market.

As a further element of the strategy, I feel it's time to place a new Constitutional amendment into the discussion. This amendment solves the problem of ever-changing law by placing the practice of a colorblind (as well as genderblind, blind to sexual preference, and so on) society into the nation's highest law. What I propose is a Constitutional amendment which simply states the following:

Congress shall make no law that codifies discrimination for or against any person based on their race, religion, gender, or sexual orientation. This Amendment shall also be construed to include a prohibition on Congress enacting additional criminal code or punishment solely based on these factors.

I added the second part of the amendment because of the increasing number of so-called "hate crimes" being prosecuted – in my mind, murder is murder whether there's different genders, races, sexual orientations, or religions involved or not. The victim is just as dead and the perpetrator just as guilty.

But the beauty of this amendment would be the phrase "for or against." In three words it eliminates a legal basis for affirmative action and set-asides while maintaining the unlawfulness of breaking civil rights laws already on the books.

There are enough issues to deal with in our nation without fanning the flames of racial tension based on outdated and outmoded laws which were created with good intention but now serve solely to divide our society into classes based in large part on factors we have little to no control over. But there are a number of other areas where society is divided which can't necessarily be as easily cleaned up with simple changes in law – instead, we will need sea changes in attitude. These cultural factors are the basis of my next chapter.

20

Culture

Back in Chapter 6 I discussed briefly what I call the "culture of life" and its impact on American society. That was part of a chapter where I expounded on my pro-life beliefs, but this chapter deals with those trends I'd like to see instilled into the phenomenon commonly known as "pop culture", and life-affirming values are one part of that.

From the days of P.T. Barnum, Americans have enjoyed entertainers of all stripes and given them hero status. All that is just fine in moderation, as are most things, but in recent years the worship of celebrity has taken too much of a place in our society.

While it's natural for Presidential candidates to carry the ambiance of movie stars, the 2008 election featured a candidate whose image was made into that of a big-time Hollywood actor with the assistance of those who work with them every day. On the other hand, Americans transfixed by celebrity had a hard time keeping the facts straight about what these politicians actually said. The best example of this is Vice-Presidential candidate and Governor of Alaska Sarah Palin having the phrase "I can see Russia from my house" attributed to her – in reality this was part of a "Saturday Night Live" spoof of her by actress Tina Fey.

Obviously Fey was poking a little bit of fun at the accident of geography which places Alaska astride Russia as well as Palin's homespun manner of speaking, but another step in the Hollywoodization of politics is the new norm for those who wish to inhabit our land's highest office to appear on at least one entertainment-oriented talk show – in 2008 we saw Barack Obama and Oprah Winfrey share their souls on her syndicated afternoon program while John McCain famously snubbed David Letterman to do an interview by CBS News anchor Katie Couric before making amends with a rescheduled appearance on Letterman's show. That trend continued in 2012 as both Obama and Republican nominee Mitt Romney have appeared on late-night talkfests.

Fortunately, thus far politicians haven't partaken yet in the overall coarsening of American society which mainly has come from Hollywood. Don't get me wrong – on a personal level I'm definitely not on the prudish side, for I enjoy hard rock music and many of my all-time favorite movies are R-rated flicks. But there comes a point where the tide needs to start turning the other way.

Compared to the movies and, even more, the rap music of a more modern era, the aforementioned tastes I acquired as a youngster are quite tame. Moreover, the Millennial Generation has grown up with the utter violence and gore of a number of video games where the object is kill or be killed, with the killing depicted in as bloody a manner as possible. It's a long way from Pong.

Then again, I'm sure I simply echo the parents of the Fifties who thought rock and roll was the devil's music or the parents of the Seventies who freaked out at Alice Cooper's gruesome stage antics and swore KISS was an acronym for Knights in Satan's Service. Each generation of parents resigned themselves to the belief that their offspring would be the ones taking America to hell in a handbasket. Certainly I have a little more faith in my daughter and her generation than that, but it would be refreshing to see rebellion more in the style of the Alex Keaton character on the old TV sitcom, "Family Ties," where actor Michael J. Fox played the straitlaced conservative son of typical hippie parents. And there are some quarters where we are seeing a little bit of that sort of turnaround.

This rebellion in reverse, if you will, is an episode which has been repeated a few times in American history. Every few generations we've witnessed a revival in American society, some manner of outcry against wretched excess. In the mid-18th century, America encountered its Great Awakening, an era where the most popular preachers became adored like the Hollywood superstars of today. A

Second Great Awakening took hold in the early 19th century, and toward the end of that century societal mores shifted toward prohibition of alcohol through the temperance movement, eventually culminating with the Eighteenth Amendment in 1919.

The latest rebellion of our immediately preceding generations came from the direction of questioning morals and authority, though. Since a library could easily be crammed full with the books written about the excesses of the era Baby Boomers grew up in I'm not going to rehash history; it suffices to say that Boomers found many new and exciting (to them) ways to rebel against their parents and their society.

Perhaps the biggest rebellion trick of all from the Baby Boomers is that they've never fully grown up. I would argue that collectively their hero is the legendary literary character Peter Pan, and that they're Toys R Us kids at heart. While those born in the period of 1946-63 flourished in large part thanks to the prosperity guilty parents gave to them – the parents having come of age fresh off the Great Depression and the Second World War – many of that generation have squandered the wealth in refusing to get old, even resorting to plastic surgery and Viagra to keep that youthful look and exuberance. There's certainly nothing wrong with attempting to enjoy life into your golden years but there comes a point where people of a certain age need to mature and realize the torch needs to be passed and good examples set. Those born just after World War II sometimes seem to be like the Kardashians of society – not worthy for the stage but craving the exposure nonetheless.

Some have argued that there's a cycle of sorts where events repeat on a generational basis, and that every fourth generation seems to face a crisis in society that makes them mature more quickly than their parents, grandparents, or great-grandparents did. It works out to roughly an eighty-year cycle and if you look back at American history the depiction can be fairly accurate.

Roughly 80 years ago our nation plunged into the Great Depression after a decade of prosperity and decadence known as the Roaring Twenties. While the previous cycle was about twenty years off with the actual shots fired to launch the War Between the States, the discord was beginning to ferment as the argument over whether new states should be slave states or free states reached a fever pitch during the two decades prior to Southern secession. The same held true eighty years prior, as in the decade before the American Revolution colonists were angered about rule by the British Crown and taxation without representation.

Perhaps you don't subscribe to that every fourth generation theory, but what is apparent in this era of both worldwide strife in the form of Islamofascist terrorism and declining economic conditions due to the collapse of financial markets and institutions is that those coming of age are going to face a world radically different than their parents dealt with, a turbulence arguably on par with those born right after the first World War. While on the surface this is a terrible fate to have to face upon maturity, in every crisis there is opportunity and a chance for redemption someplace.

Redemption can come in many forms. Maybe the youth of today will reacquaint themselves with the true meaning of sacrifice, and it's not in the form of that video game console they wanted not being under the Christmas tree. We know that several thousand young men and women have already paid the ultimate price for defending our nation's freedom, and it's a good sign that those acts which were perpetrated on soldiers returning from Vietnam have rarely been repeated on those returning from the front lines in Iraq and Afghanistan. To me that's a positive sign the lesson there is taking hold.

It could come in the form of turning away from the Me Generation doctrine of "he who dies with the most toys wins." There is much more to life than "stuff" and the next wave of kids who have to grow up with a little bit less under the tree will hopefully realize later in life that the enjoyment of those material items would have been fleeting but learning to do without helped them in the long run. Maybe the experience makes them appreciate even more those things they earned through scrimping, saving, and good old-fashioned hard work via the application of their God-given talents, and also makes them more willing to help those who are less fortunate. One thing which hasn't changed about America is that we're a charitable people.

The redeeming factor could be a return to interpersonal relationships and seeing your neighbors, rather than insulating one's self from the world amidst all that they own. There's no doubt that the world has shrunk drastically with the advent of the internet; as one example I was a relatively late convert to Facebook and it's interesting to see my friends list grow. For the most part though these people already knew me before I ever signed in on Facebook because we had actually took the time to interact with each other in person. This result may take the form of a resurgence in Elks Club membership, more teams in the local bowling league, or even just having more get-togethers "just because."

If I were to have one thing change about our culture though, I'd like it to be in those who we worship as heroes. Yes, it would bring about the loss of a tremendous number of media jobs in the field of celebrity gossip, and the paparazzi would no longer have as much to do, but as a culture we need to realize that our heroes aren't the ones portraying superheroes on a movie screen, but those much closer to home. True, when asked most rank their parents first on the list of heroes; however, it's a more truthful predictor of misaligned priorities when more people can name the latest winner of "American Idol" then name their Congressman or who represents them on city council.

In these times of trouble, there's nothing wrong with the diversion of entertainment or sports to take one's mind off the workaday world. But these things need to have their place in life, and we've spent more time living selfishly in the here and now than was good for our well-being. While environmentalists regularly preach the message of saving the Earth because it's the only one we have, I'm of the opinion that those growing up in our society need to worry more about saving a family-based way of life that's quickly disappearing.

That effort is getting little help from the media, which is a culture unto itself and the subject of my final chapter.

21

Media

In 2008, for the first time in modern history, it was reliably demonstrated through studies and polls that the dominant media had fallen to the status of cheerleader for one Presidential candidate, Democrat Barack Obama.

On the other hand, as 2009 progressed most of that same media gave different treatment to the TEA Party movement. It went from being ignored at first to being maligned before settling in to understated. Witness the "tens of thousands" of attendees claimed at the 9-12 rally in Washington, D.C. Those who were actually there and attempted to honestly count the crowd came up with figures anywhere from 250,000 to 2 million – despite the wide variance, those eyewitness accounts certainly portrayed a gathering much larger than most of the news outlets reported. And far from being an "angry mob," there were no arrests and, aside from the debris of signage segregated into certain small areas, the Mall and West Lawn of the Capitol were none the worse for wear. The TEA Partiers came to protest but left the area pretty much as they found it.

Compare that to the Occupy movement which started in 2011. Those who seized control of public spaces like Zuccotti Park in Manhattan also managed to trash these parcels to the point where vermin ran free and post-eviction cleanup cost cities thousands of dollars. Moreover, these camps were allegedly sites of criminal activities up to and including robberies, assaults, rapes, and murders. Yet they still had the backing of the media, many of whom ignored the squalid conditions to portray Occupiers as heroes, or at least representative of the "99 percent." Meanwhile, the real 99 percent recoiled in horror at much of the Occupy movement's anti-capitalist message.

Further still, it's a media who's exhibited a complete lack of curiosity about Barack Obama's background and upbringing yet assigned 11 (!) reporters to fact-check Sarah Palin's biography. And when a series of women stepped forward to accuse Presidential hopeful Herman Cain from misdeeds ranging from sexual harassment to having an affair, the accusers were taken at their word by a media which refused to extend the same courtesy to those who had documented evidence of President Clinton taking advantage of his status as a powerful member of government.

Yet while what has been termed the "mainstream media" exerted its will upon the American people in the 2008 election and continues to malign the TEA Party movement to this day through biased reporting and editing, strangely enough the ratings and circulation of these media outlets continue to decline.

The days of America's news being delivered by larger-than-life anchormen like Walter Cronkite, Howard K. Smith, or David Brinkley, read in the daily big-city newspaper, or repeated on a weekly basis with analysis and commentary from a limited number of well-circulated news magazines like *Time* or *Newsweek* have disappeared. The replacement is a 24/7 news cycle that some television networks have attempted to capitalize on through cable news channels. For their part, the print media has stepped gingerly into the online world of the Internet, desperately seeking a venue and an economic model which would keep them afloat.

In reality, biased media is as old as the country itself. Newspapers and pamphlets in colonial days regularly took the side of the political opposites of the day, the Federalists or Anti-Federalists, and delighted in viciously bashing the ideas of opponents along with whatever personal smears or innuendo regarding their enemies they could get away with. Later still, one could go to a large city (and some more moderately-sized towns) and get a newspaper which was reliably either Democrat or Republican in its editorial viewpoint and coverage. It wasn't until relatively recent times that our nation's media came with the expectation of being fair and balanced, and that standard was placed most rigorously on the newer technologies of radio and television.

Beginning in the 1930's, what came to be known as the "Fairness Doctrine" was applied to radio (and later television) stations charged with broadcasting differing points of view for the "public interest." At the risk of losing their broadcasting license, stations were compelled to scrupulously present representation of all sides of a particular issue with as equal of time as possible. If Official A came on the air and presented a 15 minute monologue on why building the new highway bypass was essential to the town and its growth, it was also the responsibility of the broadcaster to give a 15 minute segment to Citizen B who opposed the bypass because it would hurt downtown businesses or destroy wild animal habitat. Eventually, the hassle to broadcasters led them to adopt a stance avoiding controversial issues so as not to alienate one group or another and risk their broadcast license renewal.

On the other hand, newspapers didn't have to follow the Fairness Doctrine, which arguably placed freedom of the press in a more prominent position than freedom of speech. Their editorial stances were not subject to equal time and those who dictated editorial content could allow as much or as little public input and discussion as they chose to. If a letter to the editor happened to coincide with the newspaper's view of the highway bypass, they could publish it and claim there was more support to their stance on the issue – never mind the fourteen letters they received with the opposing opinion and declined to publish.

The root of much of the discussion over the role of the media was in President Reagan's decision to rescind enforcement of the Fairness Doctrine in 1987. (The actual regulations remained on the books until 2011.) No longer were radio and television broadcasters subject to having to bend over backwards to present both sides of an issue; instead they found themselves with the same editorial freedom as newspapers enjoyed.

And while newspapers continued on with their bias toward the left side of the political spectrum in their editorials and news coverage, a large number of radio stations took advantage of the growing discontent with getting a single side of the story by adopting an all-talk radio format. By and large these radio stations gravitated toward personalities whose viewpoint was conservative; with the ground being broken by most the day they signed on to carry Rush Limbaugh's syndicated radio program. Later, cable news was rocked by the success of the Fox News Channel, whose mantra of "we report, you decide" was considered by liberals to be as far off on the right wing as Limbaugh's listeners, derided by elitists as simply "mind-numbed robots."

Limbaugh's Excellence in Broadcasting radio network and Fox News have enjoyed the last laugh, though, as both enterprises continue to be successful to this day despite the regular bashing both endure from their political opposites.

This brief history of media brings us to the modern day, where the commonly accepted political dividing line of media pits the old-line newspapers like the New York *Times* and Washington *Post,* newsmagazines such as *Time* and *Newsweek,* and the television news channels of ABC, NBC, CBS, along with the newer outlets of the Cable News Network and MSNBC against a smaller but more loyally listened to group that includes a number of talk radio programs and the Fox News Channel.

One issue of the media debate has oscillated on and off the radar screen since President Obama took office. Some Congressional Democrats pined for a return to the dictates of the Fairness Doctrine as they sought to counter the success of talk radio in determining discourse on issues near and dear to the hearts of those on the Left. While they would like to see more "fairness" in giving liberals a voice on talk radio, the unfortunate fact staring them in the face is that the radio market has chewed up and spit out a number of talkers toeing the liberal line, most notably the Air America radio network that flirted with insolvency for most of its history before finally expiring for good in 2010. And while the subject is dead at the moment, there's always a chance that a new, much more liberal Congress can act to adopt something more restrictive to conservative talk radio as part of a broader, more popular bill.

This leaves the next battleground of the Internet as a Wild West of sorts for the media. And while the old media of newspapers, radio, and television all required a large capital investment for the facilities, presses, appropriate electronic equipment, and staff required to conduct a news operation, all the new media requires is a personal computer and connection to get on the internet. (Alas, writing skill is sometimes optional.)

Possibly the greatest equalizer in media coverage mankind has made possible is the technology where one can put out the word of a momentous event instantly from the scene, without an onsite press reporter or network camera. The advent of personal weblogs (better known now as simply blogs) made the idea of ordinary citizen as journalist possible; once they were married to the video streaming technology of sites like Youtube citizen journalism became a movement derided by those in the establishment as the "pajamas media."

Thus, even if the Fairness Doctrine is restored to radio and television, it would be much more of a mean feat to suppress the millions of voices that reveal all sides of particular issues. But this silencing is possible, and occurs regularly in repressed societies such as China. Even the information-gathering power of Google was no match for Chinese censors, and the resultant showdown led to Google abandoning the Chinese market for a time. Civil libertarians are among those who wouldn't put a clampdown on the internet past our current President; moreover, some in Congress have made overtures toward regulating content in the name of copyright infringement. But that could easily be extended into regulating unrelated content by shutting down an entire domain name over one perceived slight.

In the coming decades one can only dream of the possibilities for gathering information based simply on what has occurred over the last 50 years. We've gone from the days of waiting on the newspaper to arrive on the doorstep or the fifteen minutes of network news delivered from a faraway studio to news gathering that's instant, on the scene, and broadcast unceasingly. It will be the charge of those of us who are invested in maintaining a nation that advances in a direction toward government which is less intrusive on all levels to be advocates for unfettered access to news and information, from whatever the source. In turn, we also have the responsibility to be well-informed and try and sift through all the information sources to glean the truth from all which is propaganda and obfuscation.

I believe that the truth is going to be much more easily found if the principles I've gone through over the last 21 chapters are slowly but surely adopted or restored to our nation. As an armchair student of history, I've come to the conclusion that history is indeed doomed to repeat itself unless positive steps are taken to avoid the pitfalls which have trapped us before.

As my Generation X prepares to accept the torch from the Baby Boomers, even if we have to pry their clutching hands from their white-knuckle grasp around the handle – and it's likely we will have to – I hope that my generation is much more aware of the legacy being passed on to our children and grandchildren. The time we all have as controllers of our own destiny is unmercifully short, and there's always the possibility it could be further amputated because of events beyond our comprehension.

I've noticed, though, that there's a good mix of young and old who participate in political rallies of all stripes; however, TEA Parties tend to skew toward the older, more wiser generation while the Occupy movement was filled with youthful exuberance. But what the Occupy protests have in youth and energy they sorely lack in common sense, or even a common goal.

Overall I would have to say that perhaps the more thoughtful Baby Boomers are beginning to realize what they wrought is the problem and feel they have to be part of the solution, too. I applaud those who are making the effort and it belies the saying that you can't teach an old dog new tricks.

Meanwhile, another old saying holds that youth is wasted on the young. Yet it is possible that one can be wise beyond their years, and I suspect that because of the many events the Millennial

Generation have already bore witness to as they grew up to adulthood they can qualify as a group which can make more of a difference than most of our previous waves of youth could as they came of age. It's my fondest hope that if I did anything as a parent to my daughter, it was to give her as much of a sound upbringing that I could in preparing her to raise any grandchildren I'm blessed to have in a more free and just society.

Multiply that by the millions of Americans in her age group and you can see why I have optimism for the future, even with the hard knocks my generation and the Boomers before us have given to the ideals our Founders envisioned when they came up with this great experiment in republicanism called America.

Epilogue: Romney vs. Obama

As I finished the final draft of this book, we were just a few short months away from the 2012 election. So far it's been a tremendously interesting campaign.

Out of perhaps fifteen to twenty individuals who had a legitimate shot at the Oval Office in 2012, we saw a number go by the wayside before the first votes were even cast. While many had anointed 2008 vice-presidential pick Sarah Palin as the front-runner to challenge President Obama early on, she led the way by declining to seek the 2012 nomination. Others from 2008 who took a pass were former Arkansas governor Mike Huckabee and onetime New York City mayor Rudy Giuliani.

Several of those who would have been first-time Presidential hopefuls and were rumored as prime picks for the 2012 cycle also decided against running. That group included luminaries like former Indiana governor Mitch Daniels, Louisiana governor Bobby Jindal, and Rep. Paul Ryan from Wisconsin, to name a few. Of course, several of those noted above are now leading candidates for a Vice-Presidential selection, depending on where Mitt Romney wants to go to balance his ticket.

And then there were early casualties in the months leading up to the Iowa caucuses: former Minnesota governor Tim Pawlenty and now-former Rep. Thad McCotter withdrew after poor showings in the Iowa Straw Poll (although Pawlenty actually finished a respectable third, he finished behind fellow Minnesotan Rep. Michele Bachmann.) Later, businessman Herman Cain concluded his meteoric run in December after the allegations of infidelity and sexual harassment I touched upon in the last chapter. He was leading in the polls over the two months prior to the accusations.

The Cain withdrawal was unfortunate because, of all the candidates, he perhaps hewed most closely to the recommendations I make – particularly in the area of taxation. The

9-9-9 Plan, as I understood it, was a means to an end, with the end being the conversion of our tax system to one which is consumption-based. No longer could the powers that be in government use the tax code to dictate the policies they'd like to see. Several of the other GOP contenders would have liked to flatten tax rates, but few wanted to retreat from an income-based system to the extent Cain would have.

But any of the Republican candidates would have taken at least a few steps in the right direction on some of the issues I bring up. In fact, the same could be said of the 2012 Republican also-ran who accepted the Libertarian Party nomination, former New Mexico governor Gary Johnson, or onetime Republican and former Rep. Virgil Goode of Virginia, who will represent the Constitution Party. Maybe even a handful of independents who make their way onto various state ballots would advocate policies fairly consistent with the goals of this book.

In the end, though, as it has been for every Presidential election since 1852, either a Republican or Democrat will emerge victorious, no matter the protests from Libertarians or Ron Paul backers who believe their candidates have paths to victory. And it should be patently obvious that re-electing Obama would create the inverse effect to that desired, moving us away from these goals I believe are most laudable.

Yet there's a second component to the 2012 election which may be overlooked. Regardless of who is elected President, the levers of government have to originate in Congress. In 2010 Americans tossed out the hyperpartisan and shrill Nancy Pelosi as Speaker of the House, with the somewhat more subdued and centrist John Boehner replacing her. Granted, there are those who don't think Boehner is doing enough to advance the cause of liberty and there are times I tend to agree. But the key to changing that is amassing enough votes for good, pro-liberty members of Congress to create a working majority within the majority that will drive the agenda, perhaps beyond one that a more centrist President would espouse.

And while the 2006 election was a complete disaster for

Republicans, the flip side of that is, in 2012, Senate Democrats will have to defend over twice as many Senate seats as Republicans do. Even if the Republicans end up winning only half of the seats up for grabs control of that chamber would revert control to the GOP, giving them the advantage of running all the committees. However, it would take an absolute Democratic bloodbath for the GOP to get to the 60-seat majority needed to close debate since they would need to pick up 13 more seats than Democrats out of 33 contested. By my public school math, that means they have to win Senate seats by a 23-10 margin and that would be extraordinarily difficult given how many of them in this round lie in safely Democratic states.

So a likely best-case scenario for January 2013 would be that Mitt Romney has a House with a solid pro-liberty majority within the GOP which is enough to elect a new, more conservative Speaker and a Senate which would be in Republican hands, but not with a large enough majority to prevent Democratic filibusters at times – probably around 55-45. If this is the case, what can we accomplish?

Well, the first order of business would necessarily be to turn back the clock on the excesses of the previous four years and I believe there's enough will within the American people to allow that to happen. Gone would be the scourge of Obamacare and the hard work on creating a sensible budget for the government to live on would begin – no more $1.5 trillion deficits.

But just turning back the clock to 2008 wouldn't get us very far in our goal. So many people had high expectations when the 2010 elections were completed and Republicans took over the House. They didn't realize, though, that the process of dismantling a creation 80 years in the making was going to be a long, slow process, and that a key factor within that change in direction would be to have all the levers of power.

Still, the 112th Congress has been useful in presenting a contrast to the American people. While those in the House have sought tax and regulatory relief in order to turn around a moribund economy, these measures have died in a Senate which is still just as liberal as the White House. People are beginning to understand that the reason we still have rampant unemployment – which, if measured in the fashion of lumping all of those who would like full-time work with those truly jobless, would run around 15 percent – is because promising proposals to turn that around are bottled up by a party which only seems to be interested in preserving its power and not about the average American.

Yet the times we live in call for more drastic measures, ones that if done correctly could accelerate my timetable quite nicely in some key areas. (Perhaps the lone exception to that would be entitlement programs.)

In looking at the economic situation that President Franklin Roosevelt needed a quick fix for over eighty years ago, we see that the impetus behind the welfare state of today didn't take all that long to enact. The same goes for all which was added during the Great Society under President Lyndon Johnson. In life, it really is easier to destroy than to build but in order to ensure the political future of the movement the house of cards needs to be dismantled carefully.

Whether you like Mitt Romney or not, he is probably the most pro-liberty candidate who can win. That will be a disappointing fact of life to many of you reading this book, and it's likely some will feel sold out because of the previous sentence. Chances are Mitt Romney will have to be dragged kicking and screaming to the Right on a lot of issues, so it will be up to us to get in there and start pulling against the inertia of those who will tell him that the agenda I'm advocating is too radical. Maybe it is for those immersed in the culture inside the Beltway.

But the work doesn't stop there; in fact that's barely one step. The important part is being involved and pushing for things to proceed in the right direction. Fight to get the solutions I mention in this book placed into the Congressional hopper and not buried in some committee chair's desk drawer. Assure your Congressman and Senator that your continued support, both in your vote and contribution money from your wallet, is contingent on making sure a pro-liberty agenda is passed. Start on day one and don't quit.

As Americans, we still enjoy the power to make our country a "shining city on a hill." But we have to exercise it.

My book is simply a book of ideas which I believe will make our nation the envy of its world peers, something worth emulating. By freeing people from the shackles of overreaching government, we give them liberty to create more and better products, eliminate poverty by increasing the standard of living for all, and improve mankind's condition as a whole.

The masses truly yearn to breathe free, to paraphrase Emma Lazurus. I'm just putting out a road map to freedom and liberty – it's up to you to follow the path.

Thanklist

At the end of almost every book I've read over the years, there is a list of those who are thanked for their contribution and support. Mine is no different, but admittedly it's pretty short because I opted to essentially self-publish this e-book from my words rather than take a far longer timeline that publishing by traditional means would likely have meant. So, for this volume, I'm writer, editor, cover designer, chief cook, and bottle washer.. I even took the cover photo on a 2009 trip to Washington, D.C. First time I'd ever been there!

But there are some who deserve my thanks. First I have to thank my significant other, Kimberley Corkran, for being tolerant and patient with me as I follow this dream of being a professional writer. I didn't know her when all this began, but I realize now that, without her, *So We May Breathe Free* would not exist.

I also have to profusely thank those who read my website, *monoblogue*. When I began it in 2005, I had no idea what to expect from it – I was just a guy who knew he couldn't get twenty or thirty letters to the editor into my local paper every month so I had to seize the initiative in another way. Hundreds of thousands of readers later, I realize now where it all has led me.

And of course I have to thank the expanded list of those of you who have made the investment into buying or borrowing my book.

Having said that, though, it is a wonder of our system that someone like me – an author who doesn't have a pedigree or a long list of titles behind my name – is still able to find a way to place his writings into the marketplace. There's something uniquely American about the fact I had so many choices of venue in which to publish: I chose CreateSpace, but others who have taken advantage of this freedom opted to go with Pubit. Smashwords, or another of several options now available to those who have the desire of publishing and selling their works. I won't say it's quite as liberating as, say, tearing down the Berlin Wall, but now that we can get around the media gatekeepers don't be surprised if a new paradigm becomes established.

To put this tome to bed, though, I just hope *So We May Breathe Free* provokes thought into the hard work it will take over the next decades to turn away from the dusk of ineptocracy and return our nation to glory. I don't want to say "former glory" because there's still a great probability our best times may lie ahead.

It's in that spirit of optimism that I close up shop. Thanks for reading!

Michael Swartz

July, 2012

www.ingramcontent.com/pod-product-compliance
Lightning Source LLC
Chambersburg PA
CBHW070014300526
45794CB00001B/315